OPERATIONALISING HOLISTIC HUMAN DEVELOPMENT

(FOOD FOR THOUGHT AND IDEAS FOR ACTION IN THE RURAL CONTEXT)

About the Authors

Professional:

Irmel Marla

- Social Scientist & Anthropologist (University of Heidelberg, Germany)
- Specialised in HRD and Rural Development
- 28 years Head of Dept. of HRD in a German Private Insurance Company, Lecturer in various Educational Institutions in Germany
- Insights and 3 decades of experiences in rural India through participating in her late husband's research projects (prominent: "Bonded Labour in India") by co-conducting pilot phases and evaluations
- Living and working in an NGO in South India
- Member Executive Council, Mitraniketan, Kerala
- Chairperson "Dr. V. Sarma Marla Foundation"
- Chairperson of "International Institute for Research & Voluntary Action" (India & Germany)

Professional:

Dr. Kamal Taori

- Arts-Commerce Post-Graduate
- PhD in Rural Entrepreneurship
- 4 decades in Indian Administrative Service
- 27 published books and numerous research papers on Sustainable Human Development with Holistic Approach
- Co-operated and worked with diverse groups from Planning Commission to Implementers, de-centralized, market-driven, eco-protective activists, and policy-makers
- Thrust on marketing the unmarketed and series of performer's presentations for bringing out the best of individuals, society, state, and the community in the same system
- Co-operating with international institutions for world peace

Interests of both the authors:

- Commitment for improving living conditions of the neglected by holistic approach on Gandhian lines
- Establishing international networks for understanding, tolerance and peace
- Indian culture including literature, traditional crafts, arts & music and natural medicine
- Loving Nature and everything natural + committed to active environment protection
- conviction-based non-conformists

OPERATIONALISING HOLISTIC HUMAN DEVELOPMENT

(Food for Thought and Ideas for Action in the Rural Context)

Irmel Marla
Social Scientist
(Dedicated to life-long learning)

Dr. Kamal Taori
(Vidyarthi)
Philosophy and Philanthropy
in Research and Action

CONCEPT PUBLISHING COMPANY, NEW DELHI-110059

Cataloging in Publication Data—DK
Courtesy: D.K. Agencies (P) Ltd. <docinfo@dkagencies.com>

Marla, Irmel.
Operationalising holistic human development : food for thought and ideas for action in the rural context / Irmel Marla, Kamal Taori.
p. cm.
Includes bibliographical references (p.
Includes index.
ISBN 8180694372

1. Rural development—India. 2. Sustainable development—India. I. Taori, Kamal, 1946-,joint author. II. Title.

DDC 307.141 209 54 22

ISBN : 81-8069-437-2

First Published 2007

Published and Printed by
Ashok Kumar Mittal
Concept Publishing Company
A/15-16, Commercial Block, Mohan Garden
New Delhi-110059 (India)

Phones : 25351460, 25351794
Fax : +91-11-25357103
Email : publishing@conceptpub.com

Dedication

This book is dedicated to late **Dr. V. Sarma Marla**, a visionary and eminent social scientist and anthropologist whose commitment for the underprivileged found expression in his manifold researches and action plans. Most outstanding is his research and book on "Incidence of Bonded Labour in India" (published 1981). His tragic and untimely death deprived India of a Gandhian fighter against the evils of society and also, his friends and acquaintances of a warmhearted, inspirational companion. With this book, his wife Irmel Marla and also, the co-author Dr. Taori, want to honour him in a way he would have appreciated. We found his unfinished manuscripts, notes, research findings, his visionary action plans embedded in Gandhian thoughts a legacy which compelled us to take it up for realization.

He was harmoniously living in two different cultures, Germany and India, combining the best of each in his life and work. To promote Gandhian Philosophy in the West, he translated and edited "Hind Swaraj", written by Gandhiji in 1908, into German language at a time when almost nobody saw the meaning of these writings as an action plan for a peaceful world. Incidentally, Hind Swaraj is in question-and-answer form to initiate, to clarify not only the developmental scenario, but also depicts clearly the basic preconditions for a peaceful world. The world has become poorer without Sarmaji. Let us take up his legacy.

"Oh, East is East, and West is West, and never the twain shall meet,
Till earth and Sky stand presently at God's great Judgment Seat.
But there is neither East nor West, Border, nor Breed, nor Birth,
When two strong men* stand face to face, tho' they come from the ends of the World."

(from: Rudyard Kipling, The Ballad of East and West, * read: humans)

The two authors, unconventional personalities both, took Kipling's quote as a challenge to prove it and to do justice to Kipling, as usually only the first line of his ballad is deliberately quoted, thus giving a completely adverse message than he intended. The authors found their cooperation highly enriching, and decided to take up the challenge of creating an unusual book, like many other challenges they took up in their respective - Eastern and Western - professional lives.

An unconventional Preface

Why getting involved in this book?

> ***"Those in whose name we speak we do not know. Nor do they know us."***
>
> (Mahatma Gandhi)

During the churning of various literature on the topics covered around this book, we found an article in "Kurukshetra" of June 1993, titled "Making People's Participation in Rural Development" - A Reality Through Constitution (73rd Amendment) Act, 1992, very interesting and enlightening. Former Union Cabinet Secretary, Nirmal Mukarji in article "Making Third Stratum Vibrant, Dynamic", says the following :

> "On the bank of the river of national life is the over centralized Indian State, thinly composed of the ruling elites in the Union and some of the so-called national political parties. These are the self-styled "mainstream" that never tire of exhorting others to join them. On the other bank are massed the people of India, amongst them being the myriad groups that make us rich in diversity. Obviously, there must be a bridge to connect the two, but the river is wide and requires several spans. Those who wrote the Constitution built only the single span linking the Centre with a mid-point pier, where the States were clustered, and the journey beyond being left to bureaucratic boats. This first span having been severely damaged through misuse, the Indian State is left stranded on one bank, out of touch with the people on the other side. Without first repairing this span, the 73rd Amendment has commenced construction on the portion between the States and the people. The project is well intentioned but absurd. It is the entire river which needs a bridge, not merely a section of it."

The idea for this book developed during one of the many well-intended seminars on "Rural Development" taking place everyday all over the country, where it again became very clear to both the authors that most of the speakers had no doubt knowledge about the conditions in rural India. They also, had some good ideas how to improve them, but at the same time, we felt the utter lack of practical suggestions which could make a real impact.

Also, the deeply engrained evil habit of running for grants and subsidies in order to create self-employment which is still recommended as panacea for the uplift of the poor seemed to us killing genuine entrepreneurship and also, stabilising the agony of an economic stalemate.

Obviously, there is a lack of genuine entrepreneurship in our lecturers and our politicians, too.

After discussing these problems, we felt challenged to try to work on a **"Hope Model"** for Rural India, focusing on our holistic approach and, with it, on practical concepts by clearly defining the problems while including experiences from those concerned at the grassroot level.

This way, we all might get to know "those in whose name we speak" and make them **speak out and act for themselves**; the same way, they will come to know us, too, thus enriching each other through fruitful cooperation.

"But grey, my friend, is all theory!"

(from: Johann Wolfgang von Goethe, Faust)

Taking up a topic like "Rural Development" seems to be another attempt to add either one more theory to the manifold existing ones or else, to repeat some of the already thoroughly chewed through and trashed out publications. We do not intend to repeat these practically fruitless exercises but try to focus on "How to do" by underlying lessons of the past, keeping in mind the grassroot conditions and necessities and also, including experiences and opinions of the people concerned. Furthermore, we are following a holistic approach which means mainly including all spheres of life by putting emphasis on action-oriented suggestions. The main aims of the book are to actively support improvement and to facilitate the understanding of holistic issues in :

- sustainable self-employment
- enhancing productivity by a holistic approach
- rendering hope and practical perspectives to the neglected
- identifying hidden potentials
- participatory approach and action
- involving the grassroot institutions
- issues on empowerment
- identifying leadership issues

The term **"research" is very much misused** in almost all fields concerning development. It is widely used as an excuse to elaborate about wrongs done in the past. These include, for example, the lack of proper decision-making by those in power, lack of proper attitudes in the rural population, lack of future-oriented policies, and corruption in bureaucratic circles, that is, almost everything. Thereby omitting the fact that our researchers obviously lack the capacity or sincerity of doing their homework themselves, namely doing practice-oriented research and evolve suitable suggestions for actions. Moreover, even practice-oriented research is deplorably compartmentalised which leads to lack of coordination and huge inefficiency of everything which finally materialises somehow.

Even researchers working in the same fields do not network together keeping their findings and theories carefully to themselves lest somebody else might suck from the sweet fruits of their brainpower. The only exception being national or international conferences and workshops, where we can observe them fiercely engaged in verbal fights with each other, thus displaying nothing else than a most contagious verbal diarrhoea, a disease well known amongst scientists and those who consider themselves being scientists.

It goes without saying that we do have quite a lot of fine social scientists/economists and good researchers who do their work sincerely with all good intentions but also, there is not much impact on the grassroot level. And even if we find some impact, then it is not replicable or sustainable or else, it does not find adequate place in the policy-making processes.

The average citizen is mainly concerned with his or her daily life problems, and obstacles to overcome, making two ends meet and striving for one's own ambitions; there is hardly any space for thinking and acting holistically. On the one hand, society and political powers are considered responsible for one's own needs, on the other hand, there is very less preparedness to contribute to the well-being of others.

The attitude of demanding has overpowered socially conscious behaviour and the attitude of feeling and action responsibly in the social context.

This attitude culminates in one of the evils in Indian society which were purported since independence: by giving grants and subsidies and the like, an atmosphere of inactiveness, of waiting for others to help, of just demanding from others, is now rampant in our country.

Development is considered as something which has to be given or imposed, thus leading to the overkill of self-initiative and entrepreneurial spirit. To revive this dormant and hitherto massively neglected potential on every level of society, all have to get actively involved on a national scale.

In the Mahabharata, Krishna says to Satyaki and Arjuna, just before the Great War: "It is not right to stand by and watch an injustice to be done. There are times when active intervention is necessary."

The injustices done in our times lay in the fact that, in the average, still half of our rural population is doomed to live below the poverty line in spite of tremendous resources and liberalisation compulses. Hence, we all should feel responsible to take up the fight till they themselves will be empowered enough to take up the challenges and fight for themselves. And also, we have to challenge all those who benefit from these resources and the economic liberalisation without sharing their extra gains.

Fighting injustice is something almost everybody thinks right, important, and "it should be done", albeit preferably by others. Those who take up the fight, sometimes just plunge into it without proper planning or else, their enthusiasm and naivety is misused by other vested interests.

In this context, we have to keep a fine balance of our emotions, meaning a sort of "accountancy of emotions". The balancing act is between intellect (ratio) and emotions: If only emotions determine our actions, we cannot succeed; on the other hand, if intellect is exercised without being embeded in a sound emotional system determining sincere commitment, the actions carried out will lack the most important humane factor. This is why we need the holistic approach.

This book is intended to create ***hope*** by rendering practical advice and suggestions and viewing Rural Development from a holistic angle.

The holistic approach enables us to recognize chances and opportunities when they come across and also to make use of them; it enables us to actively search not only around us but also in hitherto unknown spheres. At the same time, it demands efforts and clarity for the recognizing processes and for putting opportunities into action. This is undoubtedly the prerequisite for evolving hope in oneself and creating hope in others.

> ***"There are chances everywhere. Let your hook be always cast; in the pool where you least expect it, there will be a fish."***
>
> (old German proverb)

Now, the term "holistic" unfortunately, has become quite popular as a term of fashion which dilutes the strong claim this term puts up. We attempt to define "Holistic Approach" in a clear cut way so to avoid misunderstandings and the unavoidably accompanying confusions.

We consider creating hope in all strata of underprivileged sections of our society the most important challenge of our time, at the same time underlying it with ways and means to keep up and strengthen the strive for a peaceful world for our and the future generations. In this process, the question of efficiency of the delivery mechanism, sustainability, costing, civil society, bureaucracy, etc. within a democratic system, needs to be taken into consideration. In this context, issues of confidence-building, self-esteem, economic empowerment as base of all types of empowerment, issues of emancipation in a society against compartmentalisation of empowerment issues, need to be holistically explored for action.

In this context, the term "Marketing the Unmarketed" gets its essential validity: it demands a non-conventional approach to planning and action. This is imperative, as the more the world has tried to solve the problems, the more disastrous the impacts became. The rising expectations of the masses seem to be incapable of being fulfilled by the existing conventional systems; if not attended to in time, this serious processes will unavoidably lead to aggravating injustices and exploitation, widening the gaps between haves and have-nots, and finally to the collapse of our civil society. Hence, to facilitate the surge of hope and to create a spirit of enabling environment, is of utmost importance and urgency.

In this spirit we hope to establish international networks for sharing ideas and experiences, for mutual understanding and action following

Mahatma Gandhi's **philosophy of non-violence and peace**. We perceive the term "Globalisation" as a holistic principle which encompasses local microcosms as vital elements. They have to function efficiently and sustainably in order to enable the macrocosm "global system" to function for the benefit of all and not for a privileged few.

This is the biggest challenge of our time.

This book does not attempt to provide easy answers or simple solutions to mind-boggling questions in a manner of ***"solutions instant"*** which could only lead to ***Junk-Food for Thought.***

This book provides analyses, views, models for action, and results of experiences, evaluations to learn from, and practical steps as guidelines to efficient action from the holistic angle.

It is the first Part of a series of Books on issues of holistic sustainable development.

This book may serve as an eye-opener to everybody who till now ***"pretends that he just doesn't see"***,[1] or to all those who are concerned.

The authors found lots of inspirations in books of thinkers and writers from East and West. Mark Twain is one of those who showed us how insignificant most of the day-to-day worries of individuals are, compared with the necessities of humankind from a holistic view. Also, he showed us to be aware of the dangers of a democratically structured society whose representatives are not working in the interest of society.

"Whenever you find yourself on the side of the majority, it's high time to pause and reflect." (Mark Twain)

"Keep away from the people who try to belittle your ambitions. Small people always do that, but the really great make you feel that you, too, can become great." (Mark Twain)

And, in our own way, with great compassion, we have always tried to achieve goals which others thought unreachable. And we often succeeded.

Now, we try again to achieve goals which others think are unreachable. Our motto is :

If you do not reach out for the sky, you will never touch the stars.

1. From : a song by Simon and Garfunkel. The answer is blowing in the wind......

CONTENTS

Chapter-1

Obstacles and Co-operation Issues

On the way to overall development in the country we have to emphasize that it is—on the surface—mainly government's failure to provide efficient support and infrastructure. Since independence, too much importance has been given to non-rural, industrial development with all its impediments, namely environmental hazards. But the fact that the majority of our citizens are living and toiling in rural areas, seemed to be of secondary meaning. Too much time has elapsed so that we are now reaping the rotten fruits of neglect. Of course, our citizens made it very easy for governments and politicians to follow their own vested interests which are not necessarily the interests of the majority of the people, be it by submitting too willingly or by utter passivity due to helplessness.

Of course, numerous schemes have been introduced to eradicate poverty, most of them to the advantage of a few in contrast to the many who are still suffering. Not much has been done to effectively do away with the channelling of huge amounts of money into dubious pockets and not much has been done to make sure that plans and schemes are indeed catering to the needs of the poor or else, are suitable for instigating sustainable development. The people stay put and watch everything in a more or less helpless state. Adding to this, we observe them, almost speechlessly, regularly voting for the same politicians who, in breathtaking openness, are indulging in nepotism and corruption, and who never fulfilled their promises. Our people are not ignorant; then, why do they let themselves be treated, cheated like this?

Sometimes, one feels as if there is something fundamentally, basically, structurally wrong. There seems to be an overall collapse all around; some sporadic hope models here and there have not evolved into a greater pattern or system. This does not mean that the Planning Commission or other departments of the Government of India are not aware of this problem, but there seems to be a total inability to find effective solutions. Those who have the solutions cannot make themselves heard or influential enough because the **"fraudeurs"** are sitting in the concerned positions thus hindering the entry of competent performers. This means that the gap between the performers and the power holders is continuously widening, and also, the gap between the government and the governed.

This ongoing process towards disaster and chaos has already started, not only in India but all over the world, weakening the fabric of democratic societies and thus making it an easy prey for all sorts of scoundrels and fundamentalists.

There are no easily satisfying answers to the above mentioned fact that the Indian masses are continuously using their electoral power like sheep. They seem to have lost hope long back. They cannot muster an optimistic outlook into the future and, worst of all, the disastrous fact is that their mindset is multiplied in the younger generation. Thus replicating hopelessness in an even bigger scale.

While understanding the issues mentioned below in a concretized form, it is imperative to be aware of the role of tradition, philosophy, history, mindset, power, greed, etc., as impact-makers in good or bad governance. Many feel that the government has lost its original aims, objectives and pursuits and does not fulfil its proper tasks. Now, since only singular vested interests are seemingly prevailing, it only seems to be legitimized exploiters and extortionists. With disinterested, hopeless citizens who are obsessively stuck up with their day-to-day bread and butter issues, this exploitation has become quite easy and not only repetitive but becomes cemented over a period of time.[1]

Let us now look deeper into the mechanisms of governments both, central, states and local bodies, where we find various obstacles in the way of sustainable development. The same applies to various NGOs and other agencies, private and semi-private. Some of the main causes for failures are given below :

1. An overwhelming bureaucracy[2]

- stands in the way of speed and efficiency
- intimidates people
- frightens in view of easy accessibility to government support
- enjoys no credibility from the people (whom they are supposed to serve)

- bureaucratization is a basic mistrust towards everybody and everything, thus making co-operation almost impossible
- bureaucratization leads to an overkill in (senseless) controlling measures, making efficient control meaningless

2. Agencies and/or NGOs

- lack competence and capacity to realise feasible schemes
- do not involve people concerned
- follow ideas not suitable to local conditions
- do not have efficient working patterns
- show attitude of "know-all", thus forfeiting credibility
- have dubious ways of using funds

3. Attitude of people at grassroot level is

- frustrated and helpless after many negative experiences
- hopeless due to lack of feasible perspectives
- frightened to take self-initiative
- frightened in view of harassment by bureaucrats

4. General attitude of PMO, Planning Commission, MPs & MLAs, other politicians, political bodies[3]

- insincerity in planning and actions
- lack of genuine commitment and competence in those chalking out schemes (mostly to obey and please superiors and authorities)
- choosing the wrong persons/agencies for implementing schemes
- no proper control nor monitoring
- wrong priorities (emphasis on promises made during election campaigns)
- wrong policies hindering (enhancement of) productivity
- not using potentials like PPPP: Public Private Panchayat Partnership
- wrong taxation system (and other policies concerning law-making)

From the above mentioned harmful causes which are hindering viable rural development we can clearly make out three main categories, defined after their respective possibilities for success, namely :

1. **Optimistic :** can be positively influenced with good perspectives
2. **Worth trying:** can be positively influenced but with limited expectations
3. **Worth fighting :**[4] can hardly be positively influenced, but fighting against might be successful

These we illustrate as follows:

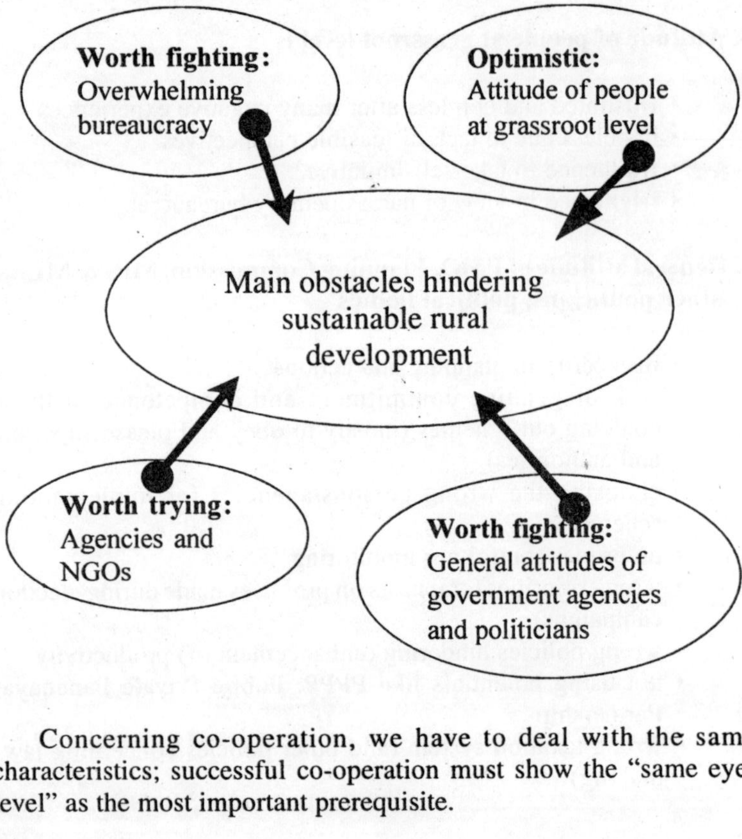

Concerning co-operation, we have to deal with the same characteristics; successful co-operation must show the "same eye-level" as the most important prerequisite.

In different chapters we will create clarity of terms used (and often misused) and suggest practice-oriented hope-plans for improving conditions of the village poor.

As an unknown author sarcastically pointed out: "**What we have to do in present times : After we have liberated the country from colonialism, we have to have a revolution to liberate us from ourselves.**"

We are still hopeful that India does not need a revolution, but can bring itself out of misery through appropriate measures within the existing system by mobilising all the hidden potentials, the power of its people.

Suggestions for Action

1. We must not forget the legacy of the Father of the Nation (for all who might not remember : **Mohandas Karamchand Gandhi, Mahatma Gandhi):** "The ancients held that the highest form of knowledge is self-knowledge and that he who achieves that knowledge achieves all. It seems to me that the value of self-knowledge holds good for nations as well. No matter how one defines a nation—and it has not been found easy to do it—its essence seems to lie not in its outward attributes but in the mental world of those who comprise it. Of the ingredients of this inner world, the most important is self-image, that is, the image that the people comprising a nation have of themselves and their forefathers."[5]
   Hence, all of us must seriously consider what we can do in developing and replicating self-knowledge; this requires as a precondition a clear understanding about the term "self-knowledge" in the first place. In this book, we cannot elaborate on this but we do think that the term is self-explanatory for all those who seriously contemplate about it. Hence, the process of questioning has to start, which we can put it this way: going from the **"I"** to the **"We"** to the **"They"**. The practical steps would be to start questioning immediately inside me and in the immediate surroundings. After that, we have to explore the "We" which includes everything I am involved in or specially interested in. The step to "They" means a big leap towards leaving selfishness to encompass needs beyond the ownself. At the same time, we have to get

rid of the concept of "sacrifice", "abnegation", "penance", etc. which in their true consequence, are nothing else than again selfish aims and objectives. Religion and Government, both are highly interested in keeping people in a non-questioning state.

Jayaprakash Narayan, in 1971 (!), put the same thing very clearly: "After the first few years of euphoria since Independence, a period set in of self-denigration in which educated Indians, particularly those educated in the West, took the lead. Whether in the name of modernisation, science or ideology they ran down most, if not all things, Indian. We are not yet out of this period. I am not suggesting that what is wrong and evil in Indian society or history should be glossed over. But breast-beating and self-flagellation are not conducive to the development of those psychological drives that are so essential for nation-building, nor so is slavish imitation of others."[6]

2. It is high time to use all information and communication technology available and suitable for the masses. This means also, **using the right to information and making them aware of how to use it.** Utter unsuitability,[7] lack of essential infrastructure, massive corruption, incompetence, lack of accountability and proper control, etc., are of course bound to a mere continuation of the same.

   Hence, small business development centres at local level with thrust on self-employment, viable investment and village planning monitoring integration is the only answer. We are afraid that with the current speed of development, this suggestion would need a long way to go if things could be improved. **But, it will be the only way**.
3. Radical, local empowerment processes need proper mind-setting. People are what they are. Systems have to be geared for fruit-eating instead of root-eating. Proper planning with ruthless monitoring and open competition, with policy support and convergence/networking can reduce the all-pervading massive wastages, duplications, double-spending, etc.—in short : we do not have to invent the wheel the umpteenth time! It is the money of the people which should be spent for the people!
4. Series of Performer's Presentation (SOPP)- from around the area in all institutions and centres would lead to an overall

confidence building of the masses. This does not require heavy investment, but by networking locally available infrastructure can be utilized.

5. Local Media : They can play a very important role due to their close proximity to the people and their living conditions, but also due to the influence they have in shaping opinions on political, environmental, social, etc., issues.
   The local media are normally not used to their potential as they are dependent on the locally existing power structures and have to support them. If the better performance of publicly spirited commitment would become the source of power, the overall mindset would definitely improve in the direction of social responsibility, thus enhancing self-responsibility and reducing the deplorable state of submissiveness.
6. Since professionals and all India services seem to have miserably failed as permanent civil servants on Weberian[8] principles, it is worth handing over the power to grassroot institutions of the people. This would be possible if the provisions of the 73rd and 74th Amendments of the Constitution are put into practice by means of resorting to Satyagraha. There is an urgent need to take up again the real Swaraj movement through Satyagraha and self-reliance for human dignity.
7. As a part of total revolution, localites have to get exposed to the challenges of our time. There has to be a radical change of mindset leading to opening to the challenges of the future and, at the same time, accepting support from competent sources. For example, by creating self-employed change agents cadres (SECAs), self-supporting systems of development would be created which could be replicated.
8. To sum up, we can say that the following mindset leading to behavioural and other related consequences, have to be fought against mercilessly :

   - sycophancy
   - flattery
   - black-marketeering
   - submissiveness
   - lack of questioning
   - corruption

The ultimate aim can only be abolishing them. Young people have to be made aware of these evils of society and strengthened to combat them non-violently. As Albert Einstein[9] rightly put it when he said that **what we do to our children now, they will do later to society**. That means also, we have to provide good role models for them to grow up into responsible citizens and not continuing the above-mentioned evils of our society. **Let us start with ourselves first doing it**!

REFERENCES

1. This phenomenon requires to be analysed holistically which will be done by the authors in one of the coming books in this series.
2. "...even God would fail in a Government office." (from: Manju Kapoor : "Home", p. 164)
3. On politicians/elections: "*under the circumstances would he enter a process of choosing the least harmful among scoundrels.*" (V.S. Naipaul, India. A Million Mutinies now, Kolkata, 1990)
4. i.e.: both: for its improvement and, against its attitudes and measures.
5. Jayaprakash Narayan, in his foreword to 'Civil Disobedience and Indian Tradition, by Dharampal, Sarva Seva Sangh Prakashan, Varanasi, 1971, p. XV.
6. Jayaprakash Narayan, *ibid.*
7. like: supplying computers in villages where there is no electricity at all!
8. Max Weber.
9. German Mathematician, "father of the atom bomb", later crusader for peace and non-violence.

Chapter-2

Holistic Approach to Development and Action

First of all, we have to clearly define the term "holistic" to avoid any misunderstanding. Hermeneutically, the word goes back to the Greek "holos" which means "entire, all, completely, total"; the term "Holism" derivated from it, meaning a type of system which encompasses all spheres, like spirit, mind, soul, body, social and economic conditions, environment, etc. This system is not to be seen as the sum of its parts, but, this is of utmost importance, it shows the interdependence of all its parts and, at the same time, has a much more efficient impact working as a system. This has to be remembered when the term "compartmentalisation" comes into the fore.

The one-dimensional chain of cause and effect we are usually applying while analysing all sorts of phenomena, cannot be applied easily without the holistic approach. At first sight, this seems to be disadvantageous, but we will show that it is, in reality another advantage of our approach.

While, with the conventional approach, we have no choice left but to follow a given line of—mostly—events or facts, the holistic approach provides with a variety of factors to be taken into account, thus broadening our outlook and sharpening our faculties for planning, decision-making and acting.

Therefore, Holism in its essence is all-encompassing. It comprises all spheres of life which can be described in short as

- Individual,
- social,
- environmental, and
- spiritual,

thus, leading to a splendid overview on the interdependencies of all the three simplified categories.

Holistic approach to action means foremost the abolishing of compartmentalisation, the latter being the main cause for lack of coordination in most of the efforts of development activities leading to an immense waste of energies and money.

If we train ourselves to look at the areas we have to directly deal with "serious concern areas", we can imagine the processes of approach as simply shown below :

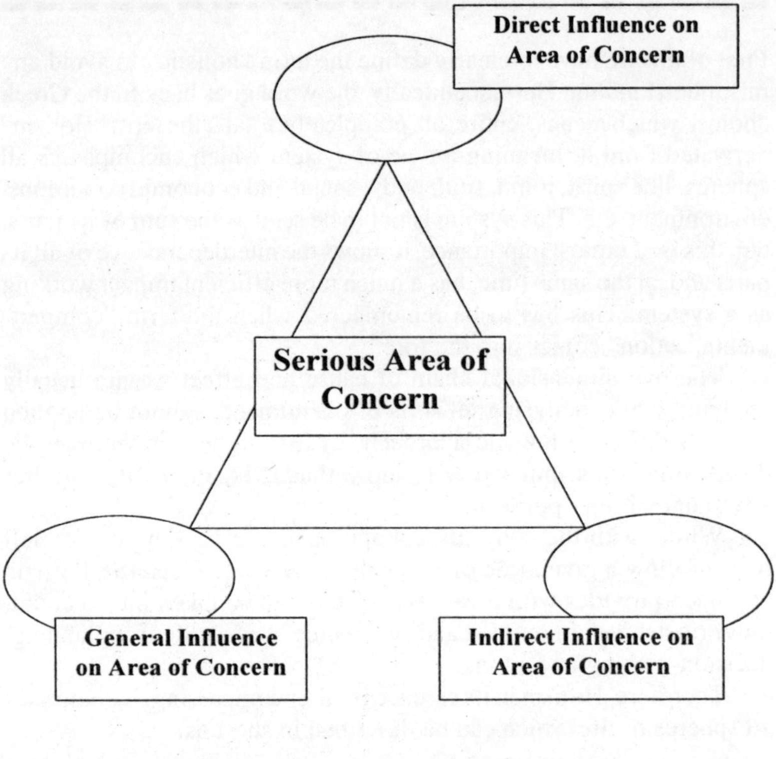

We can use this illustration as a very valuable tool to clarify and specify what is to be done exactly by answering the following questions :

1. What is the **area of serious concern**?
2. What is/are **the immediate area/s of influence**?
3. Which immediate **area(s) of concern** can be influenced?

4. Which impact might be caused on other **areas of minor concern**?

These categories we define as follows:

1. Area of serious concern

→ a situation or a fact/facts where immediate action is necessary
→ a situation or a fact/facts already harmful

2. Immediate area of influence

→ a situation or fact/facts where immediate influence is necessary
→ not necessarily action, but creation of a mindset for improvement

3. Areas of concern which can be influenced

→ assessing areas of concern where influence is possible (at all)
→ assessing areas of concern in view of urgency

4. Areas of minor concern

→ a situation or fact/facts not harmful at present
→ a situation or fact/facts where harm or danger is to be expected in future

Areas of concern have to be clearly identified not only according to our research and observations, but also by closely involving the **people concerned**. It is a widespread habit of researchers to tell what should be of importance to people at grassroot level. This habit makes most of the research and subsequent measures prone to failure. To achieve success, we have to carefully establish trustful co-operation as first step, this should determine the ways and means to be employed and again, following a holistic approach, all interaction has to be performed on an equal level, like "same eye-level" as German proverb says. Only then can mutual respect be achieved and fruitful co-operation established.

In view of the necessity of establishing trustful co-operation, we have to carefully scrutinize the motives behind certain aims and objectives. Do we deal with need or greed? Sometimes we might be at a loss to decide about, but there are surely ways and means to find out.

As an example we have to consider who is benefiting from a certain measure, or who is mainly benefiting. If it is only one individual, or only very few, or only a closely knitted group, we have to be alarmed and have to go into deeper analysis.

Holistic approach in the context of rural development cannot allow advantages for individuals or for closed groups as single goals but has to envisage the overall consequences. All measures have to be in tune with the well-being of the whole set up in a village, meaning not only a visible improvement of the human living conditions, but also protection and improvement of nature, of fauna and flora.

With this aim, we cannot continue misusing chemicals for enhancing agricultural production or, in the same way, feeding the animals with chemically or hormonally enriched fodder. Both will be very harmful to humans, too, as they will consume these artificially raised products, imbibing all the poison. Humans stand at the end of the agricultural circle of production, exposing themselves to the full force of the blessings of modern agriculture.

Another important aspect is the fact that only those have access to these methods who can afford it, thus again excluding all those who cannot.

From this example we can conclude that enhancing agricultural production with the above mentioned methods will not only lead to grave harm to humans and nature, but is also a big obstacle in the way to uplift the poor, at the most it has nothing to contribute.

Most important to always have in mind is the fact that any holistic approach cannot be thought of without the inbuilt force of **action**. That is in the true Gandhian way of thinking the inseparable connection between what is thought and said and what is finally done.

Let us never forget what is expressed in the following old poem:

Go to the people,
Learn from them,
Love them,
Start with what they have

Build on what they have,
But of the best leaders,
When the task is accomplished,
Their work done,
The people will rejoice,
"We have done it ourselves!"

Suggestions for Action

1. Let us always keep in mind that the time is more than ripe to take action, in fact it is nearly too late. This compels us to speed up galvanized, co-ordinated action.
2. This means that we have to involve all the uninvolved who may vary from place to place and from area to area. The better-off among the underprivileged, i.e. women, youth, even disabled persons have to be made self-confident enough to take their fate into their own hands.
3. Our holistic approach makes it impossible for governments, politicians and other influential groups in the society to further compartmentalize those with whom they deal or chose to deal. It is the old trap, repeated over and over again, to build up artificially groups of special attention like "women, children, disabled, etc.", in order to treat them separate from other groups, in spite of the fact that the group members themselves have almost nothing in common. Thus, the system of **confusion** is established, accepted in the society and, at the same time, serves as the excuse for all failures. Furthermore, it leads to continued exploitation and we do not see any sign of improvement which could break this vicious circle.
   Only local planning can achieve the breakthrough, as locally, the people know each other, their requirements and also their reality. They are not prone to fall into the above mentioned trap.
4. The necessity to shift from charity to confidence-building is one of the imperatives of holistic development. This means, the grassroot leadership must be exposed to challenges, potentials and change realities. It does not require lots of financial resources but a lot of co-ordination and conviction, in other words: good management. This way, we have to motivate the existing local leaders and resource-holders to

get actively involved but also to identify and develop hitherto dormant potentials.

5. Hence, the local resource holders have to be involved intensively. This way, the cost of change initiation, monetary and servicing, can be considerably reduced. This will also diversify the resource-holders to be more business-like and also, to enhance their competitive capacity.
6. To face the challenges of globalization, innovative cost reduction and marketing-led investment is imperative. The duplication of construction activity without plan for its utilization is a serious matter. The massive wastage of scarce resources can be avoided by recognizing and rewarding these grassroot performers and innovators.
7. Since NGOs have a very important role to play, it is imperative that systems of self-accounting or self-grading or self-evaluation is to be introduced. Many feel that it is desirable but difficult to implement. The practical aspect would be to expect the Planning Commission to take a lead and start the dialogue with all departments and ministries along with NGOs to implement the above mentioned control systems. Those with conviction and an urge for betterment would definitely come forward, and even put their data on the Internet to share them.
8. International institutions have a lot to contribute in the improvement process. Many have reasons to believe that systems of local empowerment could have been much more efficient when these international bodies had in fact reached the hitherto unreached. Instead, they dealt with government systems and similar bodies with all their inefficiencies.
9. The role of motivation, training, and all HRD components have still not been appreciated. Despite increasing budgets in all departments, the mindset of trainers and trainees continues to be thoroughly bureaucratic. The quality of efficient training requires close co-operation with competent, committed, qualified institutions like, for example, the IIHR, an international company working on Gandhian lines.

To sum it all up, we state that in spite of the already disastrous situations in certain areas, we should not despair but courageously, non-violently, and with openness and trustworthy approach fight for improvement in all strata of society but, most important of all, for those who cannot do so for themselves.

Chapter-3

Enhancing Productivity through Holistic Approach

As per definition, the holistic approach provides an overview and, at the same time, it shows the broader context of life, of living, in a way that is not just summing up what is there but giving additional value in combining efforts, strengths, resources, potentials, visions, creativity, and much, much more.

Holism is simply defined as the **whole which has priority over (the summary of) the parts,** at which the mere adding up of all parts does not reach the level of the whole. Thus, sustainable productivity can only be attained through a holistic approach and consequent concept, taking into consideration everything connected with and/or influencing a given situation or facts.

In a holistic approach, compartmentalisation with its waste of energies and resources cannot crop up as the specifically holistic coordinating factor is always efficiently present; its interdependent character will automatically lead to improvements in

- transparency, clarity
- flow of information
- communication levels
- mutual support
- learning from errors/mistakes
- unconv p-1 entional ideas and visions
- mutual empowerment (also for non-conformist actions)

to name only some of the main advantages.

When we take only the above-mentioned advantages into consideration, it becomes very clear that the holistic approach **adds value to all activities;** thus, logically, it applies to matters concerning **productivity,** too.

We can therefore safely state that **only** the holistic approach to development will yield efficiency and sustainable success.

The conventional view on productivity, in the rural context mainly a quantified one, has to be re-defined and re-oriented to adjust it to holistic approach and action.

Especially the importance of assessing productivity by qualitative methods is to be expressed in an understandable, convincing way.

In gross alteration of the already quoted sentence of Gandhiji, we can say:

> ***Those to whom we speak, we do not understand, nor do they understand us.***

The underprivileged, **undernourished**, and widely **underestimated** half of the average village population has to be shown opportunities to overcome their state of condition **on their own**. Those who have to eke out their living with infrequent odd jobs while being dependent on some charity for survival will have an ingrained inferiority complex. In such a state, nobody can muster enough strength and energy to fight, to take up challenges, to take their destiny into their own hands. All these can only be achieved by creating **hope** in the first place.

We are dealing here with two quite contradictory forces: on the one hand, we want the rural unemployed to take their destiny into their own hands and develop improvement for themselves and, at the same time, for the community. On the other hand, we are well aware that such a change of mindset and attitude does not evolve out of the blue. So, we have to solve the problem of giving boost and/or support by trying our best not to be the ever-helping hand, the nurse's skirt to grab if danger is there, the godfather for all emergencies, the ever-present fire-brigade.

The only answer to this problem is **hope** : if we succeed in creating genuine hope in people, meaning hope in their own strengths and abilities, not in others to bring about help and relief.

The same **hope** is the driving force for all improvements and also, for striving for a dignified life. The concept of dignity has been buried in the caves and crevices of greed and power, "dignity" confused with arrogance and false pride, a concept exclusively for those who determine the conditions in the society.

Within the holistic approach we have the concept of "self-governance" which has, of course, a lot to do with independence from grants and subsidies and also, from other's whims and wishes.

Self-governance for Productivity contains the so-called social capital as our most precious prerequisite, quality management as a mindset and the ability to take over responsibility.

These three basic elements are very often underestimated, as for example, rural workforce is taken for granted, quality management is considered as something which concerns "the management" exclusively and the same applies for taking over responsibilities, too.

We have to ask why such obvious mistakes have been made and are continuously repeated till today. What are the reasons—what can be the remedy?

In a holistic set up, we have a multifarious spectre of possibilities, of ways and means which have to be well co-ordinated and harmoniously balanced, after participatory analyses and evaluations have taken place.

First of all, we have to re-define the slightly de-humane term "social capital"; if used in a humane way, it means nothing else than the existing "amount" of human beings with their respective knowledge and skills which can/could be used for the good of all, for the so-called community. On the other hand, if we take the term as it is used very often in less humane way, it is just a heap of humans of which we can make use, or discard them, as and when it is advantageous for us.

There is also the term "human capital", which at least has the touch of "**human**" in it, mostly used in connection with business/management/leadership skills or respective decisions. It is as humiliating for those being members of this "human capital" as it implies that they can be shoved around and moved the same way as in "social capital". At the same time, our managers do not tire of stressing their attitude that nothing can be more important for them than their "**human capital**".

In all, the meaning and approaches to these "**capital**" is not really appreciating or respectful as it should be amongst humans. But the touch of **"social"** is definitely the broader one, albeit most of the time not consciously differentiated from **"human**". "Capital" means that we can use it, handle it, make the most out of it or destroy it altogether. Then, can we, in a holistic approach and dedicated to a purely humane approach to research, analysis and action, apply this term at all in the context of dealing with human beings? We are of the strong opinion that we should avoid it but, as it is, we have to introduce, define and explain it so that our readers might abstain from using this derogatory term in the future.

We would consider this a success altogether.

The terms "quality management" and also the prerequisite for success which is the ability and preparedness for taking over responsibility, are explained later on.

Enhancing productivity cannot be discussed without the term "**marketing**"; both are closely, inseparably, interlinked. We all are well aware that "marketing" can be bedevilled as a bad influence on society, especially on our children and youths,[1] if there would not be so much self-righteousness and social blindness, one could not help but the highly amused about some reader's reactions to newspaper articles. The same blindness seems to be rampant in view of the underprivileged in our society as there is more or less the opinion that they are responsible for their fate and thus nothing which concerns us, the urban and rural middle classes. We are afraid that such an attitude at least is not contradicted by the print media: the TV is a wholly different thing altogether. Like in the West, all the silliest serials are produced and screened, of course repeating all the emotionally high-pitched stupidities which occupy the middle class minds so that they do not develop any other ideas. And, most important, it distracts them from the real problems of the society, so that they just occupy themselves with themselves, a vicious circle, leading to nowhere. **Indeed, something must be utterly wrong with this society if nearly half of them are deprived of the basic means of living and the other half seemingly is not concerned about.** The impoverished strata of society merely **do not happen**, except perhaps as some exotic decoration, but nothing to feel too bad about.

Thus, we experience a slowly, secretly advancing slimming up of brains and consciousness, where there is no remedy: we can call it a **cancer of middle classes, yielding willingly to all stupidities being dished out to them in beautiful wrappings**, thus destroying not only their own quality of life but that of their children and the whole society, too. We have to stress the fact that the same phenomenon applies to all middle classes all over the world where modern technology has equalled all boundaries and will in the near future, equalize everything which characterizes a certain culture in certain tradition. Middle classes all over the world seem already to have become a completely faceless lot, easily exchangeable, with the same **artificially created needs and preferences, branded as essentials for modern quality of life**.

When we deal with village industries, or else, productivity, production in villages, we often come across the terms **"old-fashioned"**, meaning in fact **"traditional"** which we have to carefully define separately and put into the right context. First of all, we have to see when and if these terms are used so that we can find out the definite intention; the terms are so much laden with emotions, often used in a tentatively insultory spirit, for example to show one's **forwardness** in contrast to one other's **backwardness**, etc.

No doubt, "**old-fashioned**" implies a negative meaning, whereas "traditional" can be used in a way of expressing pride of or showing the inherent value of certain phenomena in a society which cannot be easily explained out of present conditions.

Now, when we consider these terms in view of our village products, we have to strongly state that "old-fashioned" in the sense of "out-moded" should have nothing to do with what we want to achieve. "Traditional" is a goal completely different altogether; exactly within the proper definition of "traditional" and without the negative implication of "old-fashioned", we find the right place for part of a highly future-oriented field of productivity.

Again, we have to deal with the term "marketing" and also, with the challenge posed by the influence of mass media, the latter, unfortunately, a widely un-used tool for our cause of sustainable human development.

It is also a fact that there is a lot to learn from many of the smaller countries in the world. The way they have organized and re-grouped their productivity processes, we have to learn a lot.

It is also a fact that a country like India with its **over-secured All India Services and other bureaucracies have hardly any incentive for change leading to enhanced sustainable productivity**. Rather, we are of the opinion that they are solid, permanent obstacles to smooth ushering in of change. It is also a pity **that our political leadership has not been able to give the dynamic practical leadership which would have paved the way for productivity**.

Hence, with these facts and challenges before the nation, we have the following suggestions and ideas for a plan of action:

1. Productivity has to become a broad-based movement rather than be confined to the National Productivity Council and its

few more or less dormant state offices. The challenge is to galvanize them by enabling the leadership to be pro-active, to network, to generate internal resources, to venture into unventured-in areas, etc.

2. The Asian Productivity Organisation with its wide network, relevant expertise and connectivity can definitely provide emerging productivity enhancement areas. Since Asia has its own uniqueness, by consolidation through existing resources and cultural ethos, better results can come. In other words: over-emphasis on Western models of development may not be productive in the longer run.
3. India has a lot to learn from the European Union. In the last 40 years, mainly due to committed, impartial, pro-active and visionary political leadership, the European countries learned to come closer and to a great extent learned to help each other. The centuries-long hardened enemies, like Germany and France, are working under the banner of the EU to strengthen their economies and help each other to face the global competition. In this transformation process, there are some important questions which, when examined properly, would provide a new insight and clarity for overall productivity enhancement by policy and mindset changes. Some of these questions include the following:

   (a) What are the challenges of globalization before the EU and their members, especially with reference to India and China?
   (b) How the EU and its members perceive problems of unemployment, IT, corruption, inefficiency, mergers, old age, common language, HRD, cost reduction, environment protection including climatic change, etc.?
   (c) What are the areas of future investments and employment, keeping in mind the opening up of the economies of India and China?
   (d) What areas of production and services will be taken over by India and China and what areas will stay in the hands of European countries in the future? In other words: which are the areas of competitive advantages and what type of HRD training, work-culture, remuneration packages, etc. would need to be re-designed?

4. For a country like India, the state governments, community or religion-based institutions, grassroot institutions, Panchayati Raj institutions, grassroot bureaucracy, associations of like-minded people and/or initiatives, local entrepreneurs, etc., all have to be involved in a sustainable change process.
5. There is a tremendous unused infrastructure everywhere resulting in an immense waste of resources. For example, government offices are over-staffed and pathetically bad organized, especially in the areas of accountability. If the Planning Commission, in the process of plan formulation of the States and the Ministries, could emphasize the urgency for return on investment, a new business-like mindset would automatically come up. The same way, the difference between plan and non-plan expenditure is absolutely outdated and suppresses productivity accounting.
6. There are many productivity-oriented, viable investment opportunities which do not require any government funds. Whether it is education, plantation, housing, non-conventional energies, sports, transport, irrigation, IT, environment protection, animal husbandry, fisheries, health, etc., are some of those sectors which require liberalisation and policy support from the government, but not necessarily financial support.
7. The role of unmarketed sectors in enhancing productivity requires a non-conformist, radically different approach. Trainings only will not solve the problems but qualitatively high-powered turnkey consultancy has to be provided. The gap between knowledge and operationalisation has to be bridged which finally forces good trainers to become doers.
8. The process of productivity enhancement is a continuous one. It is high time that instead of seminars, conferences and brainstorming sessions serious attention is paid to actual net outcome rather than inputs which is an imperative of a holistic approach. It is also important to state the fact that all the budgets spent on these activities in the last decades are documented in detail, but nothing is practically documented on policy changes or impacts. Logically, we can only conclude that in fact there has not been any policy change and/or practical impact as a consequence of these huge expenditures having occurred regularly.

To sum up, we would like to conclude that the world is heading towards disaster, in fact, it has become a slaughterhouse. The soon to be expected all-round collapse on almost all fronts makes it imperative for everybody committed to humanity to stand up and fight, but without committing the same mistakes. That means foremost to take up Gandhian methods of non-violence for success and sustainable change.

REFERENCE

1. I seriously doubt that there should be less influence on adults as is so often postulated: they expose themselves the same way to the influence of advertisements etc., and they are prone to yield to these influences as we can clearly see from their consumer attitudes.

Chapter-4

HOLISTIC APPROACH TO EDUCATION WITHIN THE SYSTEM

The educational system in India is mainly a patchwork of colonial heritage, authoritarian methods and attitudes, and business in its crudest form, shown clearly in the tuition industry. In urban areas, we find some sugar coating in the form of new school buildings, technical gimmicks, the mantra of IT on every school board, and even some acceptable sports grounds. At the same time, we have to deal with the majority of over-zealous parents who are basically convinced that authoritarian teaching methods are successful, that beating children is normal, and that the production of thousands of little parrots in the education factories will do the nation good. These parents put additional pressure upon their children by over-valuing the system of marks and grading systems, and finally, depriving them of a playful childhood, all in the name of wanting the best for them.[1] The significantly high rate of suicides of children and youth in India is definitely attributed to the educational patterns and a shameful fact.

The public school culture, one of the evil leftovers of the British Raj, led to the overall utter neglect of government schools, and to gross injustice in so far as the economic status of a family determines the level of education to a great extent. In some areas, we have the additional problem of gender bias, where in certain communities the education of the female child is grossly neglected, thus leading to future dependency.

The gross injustice in so far as government schools are neglected in every way whereas public schools—again the evil of the colonial heritage—enjoy hefty incomes and support from State and Central governments.

While holistic approach to education itself would deserve to be dealt with in a separate book, we feel that at least we have to voice here our serious concern. Education is the fundament of a society, where by our definition of education is not confined to literacy and/or being able to count numbers.

The time has come to examine why despite so many committees and commissions, no worthwhile practical suggestions and consequent changes have come up.

But, the following suggestions may help in better synergy and relevancy enhancement. This would also facilitate employment creation on the one hand and, viable investment flow, thus reducing overdependence upon the government and also taxation. Needless to say, enhancing entrepreneurial culture in all sectors of economy, including education, is a dire need of the day.

Even curricula and the repressive and stereotyped system of examination would also radically alter if the following suggestions are operationalised :

1. Let us take up those options which do not require changes in the laws, rules and regulations.
2. Involve local bodies, spiritual and religious institutions and community-based institutions to develop locally based, useful, relevant, vocation programmes.
3. Involve private school's associations in policy-making and monitoring systems development.
4. Professional teacher's bodies must take over the responsibility to supervise and monitor the conduct of their members concerning private tuition businesses beside their official teaching assignment.
5. Bodies like Acharyakul, formed by Vinobaji need to be involved in raising the level of quality of teaching, research and innovations.
6. Recognition and rewards to institutions should be based on transparency and solid parameters rather than on dubious recommendations.
7. The wide gap between basic vocational, technical, and higher education needs to be suitably coordinated by liberalization of education controls. The same way, parameters for quality and efficiency need to be fixed and applied by involving the people.
8. There have to be regular automatic corrective mechanisms at all levels, especially at the bottom, to revise programmes to suit the locally changing requirements.

9. Parents have to be guided and advised by competent child psychologists. If necessary, children have to be protected from parents who exert undue pressure. Since most of the monitoring and correcting bodies, created to improve education, have become themselves despondent and self-serving, we cannot rely on them in isolation howsoever positive their objectives may be. The only solution is a holistic approach to education which requires a total change in teacher's training and influence on parents' attitudes. For the latter, we should challenge the media to get actively involved in the change process.
10. A differentiated approach in funding, training, duration, language, etc., needs to be made flexibly functional. Hence, marketing-driven approach to bring out quality students with a creative performing drive, is unavoidable. Liberalization and setting up parameters to monitor progressive education methods have to be installed, whereas monitoring cannot be left to government bodies. There are thousands of rules and regulations for setting up schools and running them which are meticulously monitored by government bodies. But there are no rules and regulations whatsoever which demand the **bringing up of self-confident future citizens who enjoy their schooling**.
11. **The mantra of IT has to be de-mystified**. Not only the dubious practices of purchasing third-rate electronic equipment at first-rate prices, but also the fact that IT-issues are very often over-valued need to be examined. Proper guidelines in the interest of a future-oriented, solid level of IT-qualification have to be set up and monitored. The standards of the actual IT-needs and also the monitoring tasks should be left to the competent local people.
12. Issues of sports, arts, crafts, entrepreneurship, ethics, humanity, nature, traditional values from Indian ancient history, are not taken up seriously as a part of personality-building and building up responsible citizens identifying themselves with their country. This does not mean that separate teachers would be required for each subject but teachers should be qualified as all-rounders during their studies, as traditional single teacher classes like in a Gurukul. At the same time, they should be upgraded and given real

responsibility for their students, be it in overall grading up the students, be it in functioning as trusted persons rendering advice o students and their parents.

13. The aptitude for being an efficient teacher in a holistic set up is not a gender issue. It is an issue of mindset and commitment to this most important profession. The experiences in the Primary School determine the future ability of a child either to enjoy learning, to be curious and creative or else, to bear the hardships of being forced to cram knowledge into the brain without really being interested or to understand. It results in the fact that normally, only those students are topping the exams that are completely parrotized[2] and submissive.

To sum up : A differentiated approach with thrust on merit, excellence and competition in a spirit of joy of learning is required. A radical systematic change is necessary. Let us neither discuss nor try reforming the existing system as it is not reformable. And, let us stop to give the task of improvement to the so called experts, as they have miserably failed.

The only solution is a decentralized, holistic new system of education.

REFERENCES

1. A generally accepted saying in German goes like this: Parents: "We want your best." Children: "But we don't give it to you."
2. This term is to be understood as an allegory, meaning the behaviour of a parrot who imitates its master but surely does not understand what it is saying. In the Indian educational system, unfortunately, mainly this behaviour is awarded to the detriment of the future of the child, the society and also, of nature.

Chapter-5

NATURE - ENVIRONMENT

These terms build up the strongest fundamental pillars on which holism stands: when we define **"nature"** as all-encompassing life on earth, we have to perceive it as essential to life as such and derive from it the responsibility of making all efforts to protect it.

In reality, nature has been and is still exploited, destroyed, often irreparably, plundered, looted and violated in many ways. We know it, we observe it daily, sometimes we feel bad about it, but most of us do not do anything to fight it.

Very often this violation of the basis of our existence is excused as "development" or "job creating", thus claiming the privilege of destroying further the elementary resources of mankind and everything which nature consists of.

From the holistic point of view, due to the inter-dependability of all factors of life, destruction of nature will unavoidably lead to the destruction of life itself. If no drastic measures are taken, the next generations will helplessly have to bear the disastrous consequences.

From this it should be very clear that all plans and schemes for a humane, sustainable rural development have to be scrutinized after the imperative demands of protection of nature.

Regarding the present conditions in Indian society, it is to be stated that the overall consciousness on environmental issues, like destruction of forests, wildlife, is fairly developed and plays a role in the media, but interestingly, environment consciousness in the immediate surroundings of people is lacking or highly underdeveloped. We observe that almost nowhere a proper system of waste disposal is installed, and where there is something like it, it is not properly functioning, merely pathetic. There are examples of cities where their municipal corporations announce big plans for introducing systems of waste disposal, of course, not before lots of money went into the pockets of self-styled environment-consultants and the respective politicians, the latter finally have to decide about whom to assign for consultancy and, whom to assign for implementing the system and perform.

There is much media-hub and lots of functions with lots of speeches and, after some time, we realise that nothing has been done. And if things got started at all, you find that waste is collected only to be dumped somewhere out of sight, preferably in an area where the poorest of the poor are living. They would not raise their protest as they are already treated like waste.

Hardly we come to know that our citizens are demanding a waste disposal system from their administrators; some might fear the costs, others are just used to dispose their waste somewhere, even directly in their own neighbourhood—why should we change an age-old habit? Concerning the latter, it is not taken into consideration that we have to deal with completely different types of waste than ages back, as we have to do mainly with all sorts of plastic and/or chemical leftovers, which cause a disastrous pollution in our habitats.

Unfortunately, our educational system till now has not given the needed importance in the curricula. Here is an eye-opening example of a school which took up the laudable task of instigating environment-consciousness and commitment of environment protection in their students:

> I have been informed about new venture by a teacher who was very proud to convey this to me. She invited me to an "event" as she put it and I gladly followed.
>
> I participated in the meeting of the "Environment Club" and listened to the speeches; interestingly, some club members I had observed earlier on the school premises where they had no qualm to just drop their leftovers of some snacks and also, some empty soft-drink plastic bottles. After the meeting, the great "Event" started. They all donned **plastic** (!) gloves, took **plastic** (!) bags and trooped to a nearby area which was full of waste. Gingerly they collected most of the paper and plastic waste. After that, they went back to their school premises and dumped the waste-bags in a corner. Before, their group photo was taken and the club president had been interviewed by the local press. All of them were dressed to their finest, absolutely not apt to the task they were about to do.
>
> Next day, the local press celebrated this event as a revolutionary act of young people dedicated to environment protection, including group photo and photo of the school headmaster.

I visited this school a few weeks later and found the waste-bags as they were, at the same place where they were dumped on the day of the great event.
The headmaster told me after I enquired about follow-up action: "It was a great event to evoke consciousness on environment-protection, it was a great success and we had lots of press covering. But with these waste-bags, we just do not know what to do with them."
I refrain from any comment.

In the field of environment protection we see a great potential for self-employment possibilities, especially in rural areas, but, at the same time, we realise the big obstacle of age-old traditions in Indian society where not only menial labour is still looked down upon, but also everything which has to do with waste. Again, change of mindset and attitude has to be established. This will be possible by clearly outlining the individual responsibility for protecting our natural resources and propagating "waste is wealth".

In our holistic context, the topic of Renewable Energy also plays an important role: in this vast field of action we see several possibilities for self-employment, like "package-consultancy" (***Village Energy Consultant***, VEC) for energy saving and self-producing energy through photovoltaic or biomass technology, to name the most feasible. For such jobs, there is no need for qualification as engineer, but a solid qualification in planning, setting up, running and maintaining such units. The technology as such will be delivered by the manufacturing companies themselves.

The VEC will be a member of the village community and he will provide his expertise before the set up of a plant, for individual households and also, for neighbourhood plants or even bigger pools, at the same time, he will be available for solving problems after the set up.

In the same way, we suggest ***the Village Organic Farming Consultant*** (**VOFC**) who will be able to support the farmers in everything concerning organic farming. Again, he need not be a graduate in agriculture but well qualified for his various activities.[1] There are institutions, mostly NGOs, which offer courses on organic farming[2] together with training how to go about when changing the habitual farming patterns. It goes without saying that the marketing aspect has to be properly covered, too.

We should be aware that our ancestors knew very well how to protect nature in order to ensure liveable surroundings for future generations.

> "...the wild beasts of the forest came and appealed ... piteously not to destroy them altogether, but to move on to some other forest. ....Our ancestors were well aware that wildlife in the forests should be conserved."[3]

The VOFC will be able to render his expertise not only in technical and organisational matters, but also in assessing the viability and connected financial aspects. He should have good networking contacts with respective agencies and rural banking institutions.

These are only few examples for job-creation in rural areas where so much job-potential is still hidden or else, even if ideas are already developed, they are not taken up and put into practice.

Only in natural, healthy surroundings can we expect healthy people; only through healthy food which is naturally produced, not polluted by chemicals, and not diluted by all types of food-processing, can we expect our children to grow and develop into strong personalities who will take their life into their own hands.

We all should feel responsible for participating in activities which ensure nature to be protected; thus we will create society where happiness and personal satisfaction prevail over the daily struggle against all odds which still endanger the need for feeling secure, for having a decent livelihood, for ensuring a happy, peaceful future for our children.

It is of utmost urgency to take up operationalizable suggestions and put them efficiently into practice. There have been innumerable committees and recommendations for solving the problems of nature and environment protection. It is a fact that most of these committees were formed either to give an excuse for doing nothing in the moment, i.e. pretending that something is being done or else, accommodating persons who otherwise would not fit into efficient working set ups by giving them perks. Whatever the situation may be, we suggest that without any additional new committee a review of all their earlier recommendations should be carried out. This means, over a period of time, some of the earlier findings and recommendations will have become totally irrelevant in the meantime. Hence, those still relevant and pertinent, can be segregated and broken up into those of top priority, and insignificant priority. They can further be broken up into those requiring no additional funds but policy changes, re-appropriation of expenditures along with better training, monitoring, and mind-changing systems. It is a simple exercise, but we are well aware, that no government department would begin to undertake it. The biggest problem we are facing is that of an overwhelming, permanent bureaucracy which would certainly prefer to appoint another committee to get rid of the problem for the time being.

Our ruling political masters and also, the opposition, have no time to look into these issues and are not visionary enough to really envisage the future of the country. The majority of them obviously lack the capacity to comprehend the consequences of passivity in the fields of environment protection, or they have neither interest in it nor the competence whatsoever to judge any recommendation of a committee of the quality of a bureaucratic set up.

Hence, the only answer will be to consider the following options:

1. Involving the vested interests or so-called pressure points or people's groups to take up this cause for action and avoiding duplications.
2. Develop and commercialize organic, decentralised manufacturing, production, processing, training, technology, consultancy, policy-making, coordination centres.
3. Use these centres for creating self-employment, viable investment and policy-making changes.
4. By developing cluster-based parameters of degradation to nature and environment, corrective steps and systems can be initiated. Here, we have to involve the decentralized institutions of governments and give them suitable incentives for generating awareness and taking up concrete steps for nature protection.
5. There has to be passion for understanding the basic compulsions of preserving nature. The acrimonious debate between development through urban set ups and exploring an overall viability through decentralized nature-based development measures, a new renewal plan has to start. This is not a simple process but a movement has to be built up which has to be part of a global movement for peace development and the welfare of all.
6. The international bodies have to ask all their civil servants and policy-makers to understand and take up basic issues as

have been propounded by great people like Plato, Aristotle, Kant, Marx, and Gandhiji, to name only very few of so many great thinkers and visionaries. All of them have stressed the need for living in harmony with nature and finding a balance between probably conflicting requirements of human greed and the basic values of protecting nature. Harmonizing these only superficially contradictory interests has to be imperative.

7. There is a tremendous traditional knowledge at the local level all over the world. Unfortunately, the more so-called "development" or "civilization" has taken place, the more neglected these values have become. This neglected wisdom needs to be harnessed by involving various groups before it is too late. The same way as many plants and animal species become irrevocably extinct, the same way valuable ancient knowledge becomes forever lost.

To sum up : above are some of the most important suggestions for preserving nature and environment. However, a process has to be initiated at all levels of society to stop the devastating rape of nature and ensure the future survival of our civilization. If we do not do so out of our own responsibility, we owe it to the next generations.

Here again, we put emphasis on the fact that the seriousness of the problem is already well known since decades. There are enough documents and minutes of national and international conferences. There are enough budget provisions, also. But, we all know that it led to nothing at all.

Here again, the only solution is in a holistic approach to action.

REFERENCES

1. Unfortunately, the majority of our Agricultural Universities and other educational institutions do not put enough emphasis on matters of organic farming as it should be. Till now, the disastrous effects on humans, animals and the surrounding due to use and misuse of pesticides are still hazardously underestimated.
2. An example is Krishi Vigyan Kendra in Mitraniketan, Kerala.
3. From: Mahabharata, interpreted by Sri Rajagopalachari, when the Pandavas lived in a certain forest for a longer period, hunting extensively; the Pandavas moved to another place – they understood!

Chapter-6

About Sustainability

Before defining the term sustainability, we should remember a phrase from "The Laws of Manu" which describes one of the most important prerequisites to attain sustainability: **"Depend not on another but lean instead on thyself. True happiness is born of self-reliance."**[1]

As there are various perceptions about sustainability, very often distorted by some vested interests behind (What or whose advantages are to be sustained?) we have to clarify our notion of the term to avoid misunderstandings amongst our readers. If the term sustainability becomes thus compartmentalized, it can only be applied to restricted areas of action, thus losing all meaning and all practical sense.

We can also find scholars differentiating subtly between terms like "sustainable development". Sustainability refers to **continuity** in the first place, the term is future-oriented, reaches out to an indefinite future, thus playing an essential role within the holistic approach, provided it encompasses all spheres of life.

A contemporary example of utter helplessness on the side of the government to fight poverty is the so-called "Village Employment Scheme", a euphemism by all means! It is very clear that this scheme comes to nothing than a type of dole which will not achieve anything except keeping people quiet for some time.

The main disadvantages of this scheme are :

- It is contradictory to creating sustainable employment
- It does not help in evolving new skills
- It destroys self-initiative attitudes
- It creates an atmosphere of stalemate dependency
- It will lead to siphoning at least part of the money into wrong pockets
- Its implementation cannot be properly controlled
- It prevents sustainable development through artificially keeping up the **status quo**

Surely, it can prevent some farmers from committing suicide or else, it can prevent people from fleeing into the cities where they increase the population in the slums. Surely, it will suppress unrest **for some time**. But it will definitely have the impact of cementing the present-day conditions, thus forfeiting the chances to actively improve the situation.

This example is only one of so many, the most recent of haphazardly constructed so-called improvement schemes which show no visions, no creativity, no future-orientation, no real understanding of what is required to restructure the conditions in our rural areas.

> **Doles:** the evil of providing existence minimum by governmental support: kills entrepreneurship and also the will to work at all (Example: Germany!)

Here, the authors give a socio-psychological analysis through a practical example from Germany on how mindset and attitudes are determined by the treatment people are receiving:

> The last 15 years, Germany suffered an economic crisis, most of it due to the impact of the unification of the formerly two Germanies, which led to a comparatively high percentage of unemployment, varying between 5 per cent to 25 per cent region-wise. At the same time, the unified Germany still enjoyed the so called "**net of social security**" which provided a very high standard of living to all those unemployed. Now, after unification, it applied to the new states, too.
>
> It goes without saying, that financially, this could not be upheld. Even before unification, quite a lot of unemployed people in the former West Germany were not at all interested in getting employed as they had a perfectly convenient income through dole, sometimes even higher than in case of employment.
>
> This fact already led to a mindset of "let the government take care of me", instead of searching for employment, with all the adverse consequences.
>
> After unification, when the catastrophic condition of the economy of the former GDR came onto the surface, this attitude spread over the whole, now united, Germany.
>
> Of course, the vanity of West German politicians who, at that time, did not understand much of economy, but wanted to be

mentioned in the books of history, led to a hasty unification. With it, the "social net" had been spread over the new states, too. The total break-down of the economy in the former GDR led to conditions of a majority of dole-receivers, according to law.
The expectations of all those well-informed were clearly that the government had to take care of their well-being.
According to studies done before and after unification, the psychology of most of the people on dole who find themselves in a position not wanting anything, or at least not much, tends to accepting and, more so, to continue this most comfortable situation.
It is not only the problem of these people not undertaking any effort to get employed or to employ themselves, but the socio-psychological problem lies also in the fact that next generations, growing up in dole-receiving families, show the same attitude adverse to any self-initiative or else, entrepreneurship.
In the last few years, the German government had to cut down drastically all these schemes to the great lament of all those used to it, to the extent of toppling the former government.

What we have to understand from these experiences is that human nature has to have some driving forces to get things done. Entrepreneurship and a mindset of self-initiative can only be evoked by opportunities to do so.

The German example shows very clearly the adverse impact of doles given away in such manner. The so-called "village employment scheme" is nothing else than a short-sighted, pathetic try to pacify people for the time being, leading to nothing but perpetuating existing conditions, perhaps to the advantage of some politicians who are interested in winning time.

A **holistic approach** would have helped to avoid these mistakes, as it would have involved those concerned in the process of conceptualizing the village improvement scheme in the first place; furthermore, a holistic approach would have shown from the beginning of constructing a new dole-system that it will not be sustainable nor help in improving conditions. Thus, it would have led to changes in thinking and approach and possibly to a village improvement scheme which would have deserved the name.

All the money spent and will be spent in the future should be used by the local bodies for self-employment schemes, and given as proper incentives, not to be used as merely keeping up livelihood for a limited time.

The term "Holistic Planning" plays a big role in everything which is future-oriented. It represents a very dynamic element in the whole concept of holism.

If, as we very often observe, sustainability is perceived as short-term objective, misused to disguise the lack of vision and the clear view of what is required to build up a viable future for all, it is also a proof for short-sightedness and narrow-mindedness on the part of the decision-making apparatus. While the usual processes are mainly determined by over-bureaucratization, the **holistic planning** requires efficient organizational patterns of infrastructure.

We suggest the following practical measures :

1. In the process of planning, especially the grassroot planning, for a complex, plural and large country like India, the Bottom up approach is the key rather than the Top down approach. By centralized, bureaucratic, and unrealistic planning has hardly reached the people, let alone brought about any sustainable benefits for them.
2. The grant-led systems have killed the spirit of the people to put in their best leading to sustainability of the structures. These are very serious issues when one studies the holistic angle of sustainability. There is no shortage of literature on this question but where is the will and urgency to improve the quality of performance? Hence people's power has to be galvanised and propelled to take control of their life by sharing with them the compulsions of development.
3. Questions have to be put so that the challenges of globalization are properly understood and taken into account. What has been the role of technology, training, centralization, etc. in ensuring sustainability? Have some very well acclaimed programmes not miserably failed over a period of times? There are various tests of defining success of sustainability. Time, equity, replication, viability, profitability, nature preservation, etc., are some of these. Do they matter in the examination?
4. What is the role of happiness, love, emotion, family, etc. in

ensuring sustainability? Are people more lonely or anonymous today? And if so, does it necessarily make them more unhappy than those living in a traditional set up?

5. The issue of disaster prevention and management on the one hand, and local capacities/empowerment processes have to be integrated. The role of policy and funding, or even taxation and training have to be thoroughly examined and re-designed. We are convinced that in these fields, a lot of harm has been done.

To sum up : We reiterate that sustainability requires a holistic approach because globalization compels it. Those who do not bother about sustainability are bound to suffer and become beggars. No wonder, the masses will be paying the heavy price if they do not arise and awaken in time.

The choice is as straight and simple.

REFERENCE

1. "The Laws of Manu", transl. into English by Georg Buehler, Best Books, 1986.

Chapter-7

LEARNING FROM THE PAST?

For a country like India with a tremendous bio-diversity, ethnic and religious dichotomies, a number of very different languages, vast differences in levels of development, big gaps in knowledge and action, etc. it is important to understand the importance of the lessons of the past. It goes without saying that lessons of the past can be properly understood or completely misunderstood or else, not at all understood. These implications will be explained below in part B of this chapter.

The better informed systems development leads to better comprehending the compromisables, the non-compromisables, the absolute and the flexible co-operation or non-co-operation areas for improving the performance levels in the same system.

The implications of the lessons of the past could lead to a basic understanding of the contradictions, diversities, missing links, limitations, and may facilitate better planning and performance.

In this context, the following graph is to be understood:

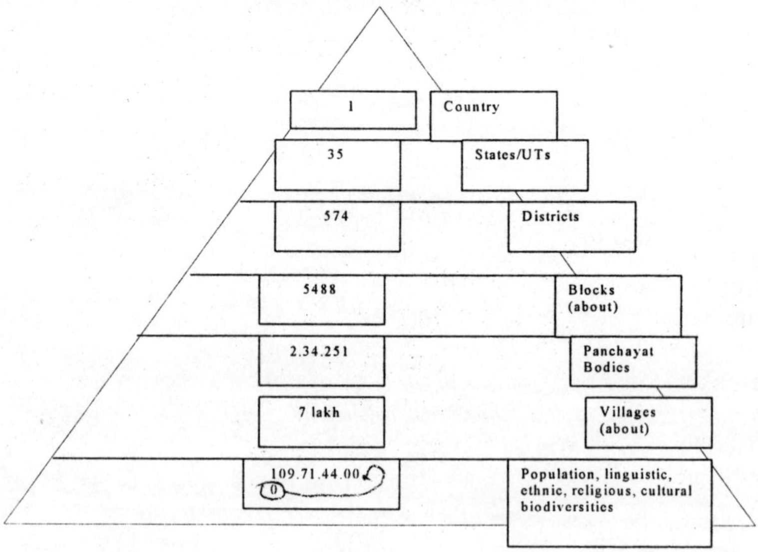

This question is one of the most discussed and also, one where we hardly find a satisfactory answer as any answer which might be given to it depends wholly on the mindset and the inherent outlook and is, also, highly dependent on the individual experiences of an individual; the problem is further aggrieved by the fact that here, "experiences" are influenced by conscious and/or subconscious impacts.

> ***"History, history! We fools, what do we know or care."***
> (William Carlos Williams)
> ***"History is a post-mortem examination. It tells you what a country died of. But I'd like to know what it lived of."***
> [Mr. Dooley (Finley Peter Dunne)]

Generally, there are **two completely contradictory schools of thinking:**

1. We should learn from the past - history repeats itself.[1]
2. We cannot learn from the past - history never repeats itself.[2]

Concerning point 1, a lot can be said in favour of this statement:

From the holistic point of view, there is no doubt that we have to learn from the past, not only the history of our own culture but also from other cultures. This logically excludes learning processes in all those who do not have access to historic knowledge, i.e. educated people, or those who do not want to occupy themselves with historic knowledge. Practically, the majority of people are thus excluded from learning out of history. At first glance, this seems to be disadvantageous to "learning from history", but we can also interpret it as a protection against various misinterpretations provided those who draw lessons from history are doing it truthfully and also, disseminating their findings according to truthful analysis.

We can safely state that the phenomenon of repetition of historic events are definitely existing, albeit adjusted to respective social and cultural conditions and also, conditions in the natural surroundings like natural calamities, climatic change, etc. Sometimes, we find it extremely difficult to transport historic events and human behaviour in our time by comparing them with contemporary conditions, but still, as the patterns of human behaviour have basically not changed much from stone-age times, it is always worth learning from.

We might be very proud of all the achievements mankind has gained since the stone-ages, but in reality, our behavioural patterns remained the same: urge for safety from dangers (one's own and also, one's kith and kin, or tribe, or nation), for procreation, for possessions, for power, to name only those criteria which had the strongest impact on human behaviour and still have. We still do not mind to go to the extent of killing other human beings on the pretext of otherwise being endangered; we still have the same mental/physical mechanisms to produce the necessary hormones in order to secure procreation of mankind; we still crave for all sorts of possessions which are not necessary for our survival or happiness; and, combined with the crave for possessions, we crave for superiority over other human beings and also, over nature, through various means.

In this view, mankind indeed could and should learn their lessons from history, even if it might not repeat itself in the identical way.

If we search the answer to the question "Can we learn from the past?", then it has to be: yes, we can, yes, we should. It might prevent us to repeat the same mistakes over and over again.

Concerning point 2, **it is what we perceive as reality** which leads to this statement. Even those learned scholars, researching and interpreting historic events, do so mostly by filtering their findings and inducing their own opinions into it. This way, history is of course not repeating itself as we can find various very different descriptions and analyses of the same historical event.

What counts should be the basic facts on the one hand, and the reactions of people on the other hand, both seen from the angle of human behavioural patterns as explained above.

Very often, keeping up certain traditions is confused with "old-fashioned" which is, of course, a gross mistake in approach, considering the fact that it is bare from logical thinking and also, neglecting the fact that our ancestors new so much more about nature and how to protect it than we do, because they practically lived much closer to nature, they were well aware that their lives and their future depended on it. They considered themselves an integral part of their surroundings and were conscious about harming nature is the same as harming themselves.

We offer the following suggestions:

1. We need a cadre of Self-Employed Change Agents (SECA) and a suitable organisational structure to regularly train and use them.

2. We must integrate with Rural Infrastructure/Investment Galvanising Services (RIIGS), suitable changes in the funding systems for rural clusters are also required.
3. Developing new products and marketing requires a new mindset, attitude and visions with action plan.
4. Marketing the Unmarketed in all aspects becomes the key word in operationalising holistic planning.
5. Area to area, schools, colleges and local bodies, have to be involved to prepare lessons of the past which cannot be left to government servants.[3]

REFERENCES

1. "If the past has been an obstacle and a burden, knowledge of the past is the safest and the surest emancipation. (Lord Acton)
   "There is no history of mankind, there is only an indefinite number of histories of all kinds of aspects of human life." (Karl Popper)
   "History is philosophy teaching by example and also by warning." (Lord Bolingbroke)
   "History teaches everything including the future." (Lamartine)
   "If you would understand anything, observe its beginning and its development." (Aristotle)
   "A country without a memory is a country of madmen." (George Santayana)
   "History is the self-consciousness of humanity." (Droyson)
   "History cannot give us a program for the future, but it can give us a fuller understanding of ourselves, and of our common humanity, so that we can better face the future." (Robert Penn Warren)
   " The past is always a rebuke to the present." (Robert Penn Warren)
2. "History consists of a series of accumulated imaginative inventions." (Voltaire)
   "Imagination plays too important a role in the writing of history, and what is imagination but the projection of the author's personality." (Pieter Geyl)
   "History is now strictly organized, powerfully disciplined, but it possesses only a modest educational value and even less conscious social purpose." (J. H. Plumb)
   "History is something that happens to other people." (source not known)
3. See chapter "Holistic Approach to Education within the System", p. 12.

Chapter-8

MINDSET AND ATTITUDES

Attitudes are determined by the **mindset**; we should be well aware of the fact that it is highly difficult to :

(a) assess the mindset of a person or, for that matter, mindsets within a group or community,
(b) influence it towards change in a sustainable way,
(c) assess if a mindset is genuine or, if it is adopted from one or various individually chosen role models.

The term "mindset" is subject to various definitions, dependent on the specific framework in which it is dealt with. From our holistic approach, we define it basically as a **mental attitude which determines the way a person (or a group) interprets or respond to given situations**; thus, it determines :

- the way of thinking or the thought processes
- the characteristic patterns of behaviour (including language)

Furthermore, in our context, we explain it as follows:

- our mindset helps us avoiding "re-thinking" every time we come across the same or else, similar situations
- our mindset transfers contents into different layers of our mental spectre automatically; we could broadly call this phenomenon "learning from experiences"
- our mindset, being a closed system, helps us to identify and structure knowledge and experiences[1]
- the mindset of individuals or groups is often modelled after external inputs through role models or so-called power groups (like religious or political influences, fashion, phenomena like anti-Semitism in Germany, the opinion of the majority of US citizens at the beginning to the Iraq war, or communal riots in India, just to name a few examples of many).

Now, if we look more closely at the term "**Mind-Set**", we associate with it a certain **closed system of thinking** which determines mainly one's outlook to life and one's actions; thus, one's attitude towards the way of life is also determined by it. Logically, a person's so-called "character" is also highly determined by it, depending, of course on some other factors like temperament, physical conditions, et al. (and others), whereas the so-called psychological set up is closely interlinked with the mindset. In a negative set up, they can determine each other in a vicious circle which can end up disastrously for the personality as a whole.

Why do we observe these processes uniformly more often than previously, not only in Indian society but all over the world. Albeit, we should put special emphasis on these phenomena in a country like India where the polarization of society is becoming sharper and sharper, thus brutalizing conditions and, with them, the mindset, tremendously. The only option in such a situation would be to establish more transparency, accountability, mass quality education and an attitude of "**striving for excellence**" in practice. In all, there has to be "**good governance**" in every field of society.

Again, in our context, we have to consider how to change the mindset of people in a direction which will empower them to take their life into their own hands, to develop self-confidence and self-initiative, to find out and develop their hidden potentials. From the viewpoint of the neglected people in our villages, we can state: after having experienced suppression, want, disapproval by the society and the like, a veil of hopelessness has shrouded the minds. It is to be the foremost task to break through this **barrier of hopelessness**, this web of fatalistic inaction by creating hope. A person who is constantly struggling with the problem of satisfying the most elementary needs like food, clothing and shelter has no mindset to listen to suggestions how to improve his life. On the contrary, he has experienced again and again that all promises have been broken, especially those made by official authorities. Why should he put trust in another attempt by people who have nothing to do with his plights? Why should he make efforts if—after all practical experiences—nothing with materialise in the end?

Creating hope means creating trust on the one side, and **credibility** on the other; trust in one's own abilities and potentials, credibility in people who offer support. The latter are unfortunately very often, for different reasons, not suitable to instil sustainable development; the main reasons are the following:

- lack of convincing communicational abilities
- lack of genuine commitment[2]
- lack of proper expertise
- lack of stamina to accomplish a work once begun
- lack of ability or preparedness to adjust to different people and (living) conditions
- lack of ability to focus on aims and objectives once decided upon[3]
- lack of dealing with actual problems and/or failures
- lack of flexibility and creativity in mind and action
- lack of comprehending the difference between loyalty and sycophancy.

We have to be self-critical enough to analyse the results of our work according to the above-mentioned criteria so that we might shoulder tasks for which we are not equipped in mind, body and soul.

> ***"Every worthwhile accomplishment, big or little, has its stages of drudgery and triumph; a beginning, a struggle and a victory."***
> (Mahatma Gandhi)

The stamina to hold on to tasks people have decided to take up, even when they have to struggle hard with problems and many unforeseen difficulties, has to be built-up in the individuals. Only then can success be felt as a personal achievement, the latter leading to enhanced self-confidence and self-empowerment. A victory which falls into our lap just like that, shying away from real efforts, fleeing before obstacles, even when they are not yet erupted, thus depriving themselves from gaining (job) satisfaction.

As explained in the elaborations about Nature and Environment, learning from the past is not restricted only to related experiences in the near past, but we can learn a lot from our ancestors, who knew many things much better as we do, who were much more conscious about their responsibilities in society and also, towards nature. We learn that they obviously had to deal with exactly the same problems caused by mindset and human behaviour as we do in our most modern world. Taking over responsibility, being self-initiative, putting efforts into work, never went without saying and had to be evolved in most of the people, like we have to evolve these attitudes and activities in ourselves and in our sisters and brothers.

> "The Gods grant boons to foolish people who persistently practise penances, as intoxicants are sold to fools for money. They lead to loss of self-control, and this leads to the warping of the mind and utter destruction."[4]

"Striving for excellence" as a Mindset—as opposite to the *"Just-so-Syndrome"*

By observing attitudes to work and also, performance, we come across a phenomenon widespread in India which we like to call the "**Just-so-syndrome**" (or "Magnana"—syndrome[5]). It is defined as a way of performing by putting in the minimum effort, not caring for durability, practicability, customer-satisfaction, in short: overall quality. A French proverb expresses this attitude "Après nous, le deluge", meaning: After that, floods may come, or, after a German proverb "Out of sight is out of mind", expressing the same attitude of not caring what may happen after a product is out of hands.

This attitude can be **exemplified**, giving only a few, really classical, cases of many[6] :

1. **Kitchen utensil** with a handle, a pan; the handle is fixed with a single screw which is too short. This leads to the following difficulties the customer has to deal with:

    - the handle can never be properly fixed (a single screw is not enough!)
    - the handle is always loose and wobbly (dangerous while working with the product)
    - after a shortwhile, the handle breaks at the joining point
    - the product becomes useless

2. **Garments**: they are stitched so narrowly at the seams and the joint, that very soon the seams disintegrate, leading to another "Just-so" effect on the side of the customer who does not care to properly mend it (of possible at all), but resorts to

fixing it with pins and similar things. If you observe people closely, you sometimes get the impression that they, while having so many pins and needles on them, will be whooshing to any magnet in their vicinity.

3. **Telephone Service:** Telephone connection is not functioning, the workers promise to come at the earliest, within the next one to two hours :

   - after the whole day goes by, no worker turns up
   - next day: repeated calls (from neighbour's telephone), repeated promises, but no worker turns up
   - next day: complaint to the Customer Service, the day goes by without workers turning up
   - next day: mail to the office of the General Manager describing the situation
   - same day: workers come and do the repair work.

4. **Dhobi Service:** he promised to deliver within 3 days :

   - he has not delivered after 5 days
   - he does not inform about the delay
   - somebody is sent to inquire
   - dhobi promises to deliver next day
   - he does not turn up
   - somebody is sent informing him that another dhobi will take over
   - next day, dhobi delivers.

These examples could be continued endlessly, as we all are suffering by these attitudes; it shows clearly that the mindset is not at all customer-oriented, but negligent and self-centred.

We will not go deeper into the widespread problem with time-consciousness, i.e. with punctuality. Only this much: a German proverb says: "Punctuality is the politeness of kings." Essentially, lack of punctuality is nothing else than utter disrespect towards fellow-beings, as there is no concern about inconveniences it creates and also, no realisation that precious time is stolen from others. In this context, lack of punctuality even oversteps the "Just-so"-syndrome, as lack of respect towards others shows a deficiency in character, too.

The "Just-so"-syndrome is, at the same time, unfortunately strengthened by the much too reluctant reaction of the victims themselves. They react usually with a lot of hue and cry, of complaining to all and sundry but not directly to those who are responsible for the sufferings. This is a waste of time, spoiling the day, and also, perpetuating the habits of negligence in the culprits.

When dealing with attitudinal patterns in order to change them, we have to keep in mind that we have to tackle not the problem of how to get innovative thoughts in the minds by, for example, strengthening willpower and the like, but to see to it that we induce the **mental preparedness for change**. This can only be achieved by strengthening self-confidence and hope.

The *"Carrier-of-doubts"*-Syndrome

We all come across this "Carrier-of-doubts"-Syndrome quite frequently, and unfortunately it seems to be a highly contagious disease. In short, we could also call it the well-known **"Yes-but"-Syndrome**, but the previous term describes much more precisely the fact, that the disease is closely related to an individual's mindset. An individual affected by this disease is basically frightened, not prepared to take over responsibility, he tries to hide this and compensates by showing *extra expertise* in expressing *extra serious* doubts, like "This will create insurmountable difficulties", "We already tried this earlier, but unsuccessfully", "Do you really mean to take such a huge risk?", etc. Or, putting up the age-old armour against all innovation, creativity, and progress: "But we always did it this way" with its twin "It was *never* done like this", meaning that everything should stick to the *status quo*. Thus, he tries to impress with his expertise in expressing his (pseudo) opinion, whereas in reality, he does not incur any obligation but succeeds in cementing things like they are, and he feels safe.

Unfortunately, those behavioural patterns are widespread in administration and other areas where decision making can be dragged down to non-performance without any consequences.

In the practical field where action is required, it all comes down to the wonderful technique of **making possibilities impossible**.

How can we deal efficiently with these attitudes? How can we bring about the necessary change in the mindset?

It all depends on the bundle of factors[7] which lead to a given individual (or group) mindset; those factors[8] can be

- Inferiority complex
- Failures in performance
- Failures in attaining aims and objectives
- Lack of job satisfaction
- Misanthropic outlook to life.

We have to stress again: creating a holistic attitude to work performance would do away with all these obstacles. We have to re-define the term **"excellence"** or **"striving for excellence"** in a practical way so that it is not perceived as something far-reaching, not attainable, and exclusively meant for a few highly talented lunatics.

"Striving for excellence" in this view means nothing else than a mindset which is focused on a quality—and production-oriented approach to work and also, to social patterns. Approaching people, communicating, is a way of production, too, the products being contacts, relations between humans; these relations determine our whole life and thus, the quality aspect is of utmost importance.

Gandhiji's Talisman

> "I will give you a talisman. Whenever you are in doubt or when the self becomes too much with you, apply the following test : Recall the face of the poorest and the weakest man whom you may have seen and ask yourself if the step you contemplate is going to be of any use to him. Will he gain anything by it? Will it restore him to control over his own life and destiny? In other words, will it lead to *Swaraj* for the hungry and spiritually starving millions?
>
> Then you will find your doubts and yourself melting away."

To sum up, the authors, with their long experiences as public-spirited service and professional, put emphasis on the following points :

1. Better informed and committed leadership which willing to continuously learn can definitely facilitate better mindsets and attitudes and thus, a better informed society.

2. Positive thinking and trying to locate positive performers around local conditions do not require grant-based efforts and subsidies but only thorough, serious searching around. This means, with a keen eyesight and determination, it is possible to trace good performers in the same system that have a positive mindset and attitude.
3. There are enough examples where people with a perverted, sadistic mindset changed their attitudes when being convinced through better experiences. Hence, we can say: it is the bitter or better experiences which ultimately lead to the formation of mindsets and attitudes.
4. We have to continuously make aware and propagate the truly holistic method of "**making the best out of everything**", even out of a severe crisis situation, instead of wasting time and energy for self-pitying or complaining. The latter, as we all very well know, leads to further deepening an already bad situation.
5. One of the authors, Dr. Kamal Taori, in his book on disaster management, has given many feel-good-factor facilitators which would facilitate the enabling of an atmosphere to more efficiently cope up with disasters in a right mindset.
6. Since an enabling atmosphere or societal climate would have to go a long way, in order to speed up the process, we suggest of having regular presentations by series of performers. This has to be systematized, and a model for systematic performance has to be developed on practical holistic lines.

REFERENCES

1. The level of structured mindset determines our way of thinking like being able to switch between either static or dynamic thinking, i.e. focusing on something or hopping from one thing to the other; the same way, our ability to reflect on things, to meditate, or to grasp ideas quickly, are mainly dependent on the structure or the mindset.
2. These are the "Do-gooders", the "Know-alls", those who want to show off their charitable character, those who have their own vested interests (like politicians), those who have just nothing else to do, etc.
3. A very common weak spot in self-styled leaders which can be easily observed as lack of organisational abilities.
4. From: Mahabharata, interpreted by Sri Rajagopalachari, Bharadwaja to his son Yavakrida.
5. "Magnana" (Italian, for: "tomorrow"; it actually means that something is put

off at least for the time being, shifted not only to "tomorrow" but indefinitely, too.

6. All examples are authentic, personal experiences.
7. Selected factors are shown as examples.
8. Factors can be observed as randomly combined clusters in individuals.

Chapter-9

The Role of Media in Creating Mass Mindset and Attitudes

The role of mass media is researched extensively; the findings are used in various fields by all people and groups who want to take advantage of them. As in all spheres of mass psychology, the "good" and the "bad" influences are widely discussed, are judged, and not only verbal fights are taken up when self-styled guardians of truth and morals step in. We can remind of some tragic examples like whipping up enmities within communities by vested political interests, like widespread uproar when an actress speaks out about common sexual behaviour, known as reality by everybody, but anxiously kept under the carpet.

Especially the vast middle classes with their regular access to mass media—newspapers, magazines, radio and TV—determine almost completely the topics the journalists should take up. The editor of a well known weekly in India said that it is the middle classes where the journalists are recruited from, they are also the buyers and subsequently, they determine what is to be printed, broadcasted and screened. He very openly stated that it is "middle classes taste" which determines the topics publicly taken up and discussed. This results logically in overblown pseudo-important issues and a sugar-coating of the real problems the Indian society as a whole has to face, thus doing away with any guilt consciousness which otherwise might come up.

The best example in this context is to be seen in all the glossy so called women's magazines. Here, the layout and many topics convey the impression of forwardness, even women's empowerment, etc. But in reality, nothing else is conveyed than traditional values in the sense of keeping women to their traditional roles as housewives and servants in this male-dominated society. The message is very clear: if women become more fashion-oriented **(even if the introduction of Western style clothing is not only pathetically clumsy but also not practical**

in this climate), try out international cooking recipes **(keeping them even longer in their traditional role as food-providers than with more healthy Indian dishes),** decorate their houses in Western style (**not suitable to the climate and also, mostly pathetically ugly**), etc., they are considered "**modern**". The message is conveyed that a woman who is allowed to work and pursue her professional career can do so because of the generosity of her husband; nowhere is it stated that the husband is clearly taking advantage of the additional income as it is still he who decides how to invest the money. The women's magazines are full of tear-jerking stories the like of "How I saved my marriage"—of course, by gladly sacrificing career or taking up cooking courses, or something else, "How I gained the love of my in-laws" —of course, by happily submit to views and habits of those, etc.

All these messages are cementing the present state of affairs, induce a fear of change and isolate the Indian middle classes from the needs and problems of their fellow citizens. Being "modern" is supposed to be good and it means, being Western oriented but backwardly traditional; being simply "traditional" is supposed to be bad, as it conveys the message of "Indianness" which is unwanted.

Basically, it all comes up to what is profitable and what is not, those who have buying powei want to shape the society.

Here, we clearly see the crucial point: what is determining or who determines what is "good" or "bad"? Is it determined by the overall (i.e. majority) norms of the society? And what, we have to stress, determines practically these norms? How do we define the so called "value system" of a society?

We all agree that an existing value system with its norms, restrictions and also, suppression, is determined by the majority of people in a society who follow these. This academic view might function in closed socio-economic conditions, it is a simplified view which might be applicable to fairly homogeneous societies, but this way, we cannot do justice to Indian conditions.

In a multi-cultured society like India, theoretical umbrella tools like "social norms" and "value systems" of the society cannot lead us anywhere near practically useful perceptions. We are confronted with a multitude of very different communities, having their own distinct norms, values and subsequent patterns of behaviour. The above-mentioned aspects of influence of middle classes on media and their subsequent dominance in certain spheres of life, is worlds apart from areas in India where the middle classes and their upcoming have had no impact as yet.

On the one hand, the mass media with their advertisement-based programmes influence those who expose themselves to them, in a regular way mainly the middle classes, they create needs and aspirations and determine mindsets and attitudes of several generations. On the other hand, the middle classes themselves influence the editors and the advertisement-oriented marketing experts in providing them with everything according to their taste. Indeed, a vicious circle!

On this background, the influences of Media on mindsets and, consequently, on changes in behavioural patterns, can be very different, as the same "messages" will be perceived quite differently by different people with their distinct cultural background and actual patterns of individual behaviour and social norms.

It is very easy, very superficial, to blame the mass media for all sorts of evils in society, for the break-up of traditional values; there is definitely some influence, be it strong or weak, or permanent, but putting the blame on Media as such for "unwanted" changes in society is nothing than an excuse for letting it happen. **Media business is business, meaning that they convey those messages which they can easily sell!**

This leaves us with the only possible answer: Let us **use** the Media for our cause. It is a widely untapped resource for powerful support.

To sum up, we are giving some ideas for operationalising change with the active support of the media:

1. A climate of positive attitude has to be encouraged at all levels of policy-making, training, research and documentation.
2. Rewards and incentives for those writing hope-generating articles but not suppressing the facts of life should be given. This means, the problems and adverse facts have to be clearly shown but with a constructive outlook.
3. The rural media need better organisation to work with grass-root institutions of governance. For this, regular information circles have to be set up.
4. Suitable local media have to be created to facilitate networking of local entrepreneurs (IT solutions) and also, to facilitate a high level of information at all levels.
5. Information tours,—travels and—programmes for the local media but also for a wider spectre like TV channels, have to be planned and organized.
6. The media as catalysts for sustainable development need to

be activated. This should be started by identifying responsible, committed journalists and involving them actively in the programmes. It can be done in the form of regularly monitoring the development of a certain scheme or else, by making the media a part of a scheme, for example as mediators for external contacts.

7. Regular brainstorming with local media by involving all stakeholders would be of great advantage in overall improvement of communication and understanding of different partners and also, would-be partners.
8. The most important question which arises in all operationalising issues: **who will takeover and implement the necessary steps?** Why should he/she/they do it?

   We are of the opinion that only the individuals and groups concerned can takeover these tasks, as only they know about their own needs and their demands, only they can express them properly and precisely, and only they can build up a trustful way of sustainable co-operation. This way, the people concerned have their vested interests in this co-operation.

   But why should the media get involved? This question is very easy to be answered: because they benefit immensely from it; be it by more professional, actual journalism, be it by doing justice to their underlying consciousness of having responsibilities in view of the welfare of the civil society, or be it merely for performing good marketing in view of future customers.

Chapter-10

Potentials and Attitudes, Role of Trainings

Dealing with human attitudes, we have to state that it can best be explained from the holistic angle as the individual view on everything concerning his own being is determined by a vast variety of very different factors of which we can only give some examples, like :

- conditions and experiences in early and later childhood (family background),
- conditions and experiences during youth and adulthood,
- successes and failures,
- role models,
- aims and aspirations,
- chances and perspectives,
- education, spiritual life,
- love and affection received,
- social contacts and communication, community,
- responsibilities,
- status, living conditions,
- surroundings (rural, urban),
- language,
- etc.

We can easily understand that by trying to assert somebody's attitude to life and work, it seems to be an uphill task. To make it easier, let us concentrate on "result"-factors which can be observed and categorized.

What we observe today is very often an attitude of demanding only instead of self-initiative working for one's own goals or for society. In our context, the main reason lies in the fact that for too long development has been understood and acted upon as something to be done from outside, as government's responsibility, as voluntary help from outside, being granted, given by governmental or non-governmental or other sources, thus suppressing, killing the upcoming of self-responsibility and the self-fulfilment which can only be achieved by one's own efforts. This mindset and attitude is one of the main evils to be tackled when sustainable development should be achieved, and it is one of most difficult problems to be solved, as it concerns the whole mindset. Changing a mindset is an uphill task and it has to be dealt with utmost care and insight.

In our context, we have to specially look into the problem of "attitude to work"; what is often considered as "lazy" or "indifferent" and the like, should not be judged in this high-handed manner but carefully analyzed. Soon it is to be found that the vast majority of people are eager to work if they see any perspectives in doing so; it is basically a matter of self-esteem and dignity which is important for everybody.

> ***"Satisfaction lays in the effort not the attainment. Full effort is victory."***
>
> (Mahatma Gandhi)

We would all agree with the Mahatma, even when often facts and observations need not necessarily lead to this opinion.

But as soon as proper perspectives in life through work are acknowledged, it becomes an undeniable fact. We can rely on this phenomenon of transformation of mindset and attitude which will help us to decide on the best steps and methods to be applied.

The assessment of one's ability or suitability for a certain task or job has to start from the "result" we expect; that is: top to bottom first. We have to clarify our expectations and derive from these the necessary characteristics (work ability profile).

By focusing on practical aspects of rural development, we naturally have to restrict our views on certain topics; vast fields like phenomena in human psychology can only be dealt with in our given framework: action-oriented. The practical side of it lies simply in **result-orientation** in contrast to process-orientation, the latter leading to no results at all.

Evolving hidden potentials requires a systematic overhauling of widely trodden paths under following deliberately (thought) provoking challenges :

- Educate the Educationists
- Learn from the so-called Un-learned
- Market the Un-Marketed
- Recognize the Un-Recognized
- Organize the Un-Organized
- Un-Train and Train the Trainers
- De-Politicize and Politicize the Politicians
- De-bureaucratize the Bureaucrats
- Civilize the Civilians/Citizens
- Humanize the Humans

These have to be postulated in close connection with the following issues which have to be taken up and dealt with under the holistic approach:

1. ***Research and development in decentralized sectors:*** In close connection with each other, results of research in changes and/or developments in certain areas have to be taken up and evaluated in an action-oriented way. The factor of decentralization has to be scrutinized and given special attention in all the following practical suggestions. It goes without saying that in every step the local people and institutions must contribute in every aspect possible. Their contribution can be in terms of money, knowledge, time, expertise, resources, infrastructure, contacts, demonstrations, etc.; the most important factor being the practical involvement.
2. ***Gurus and the context of regionalism, ruralism, urbanism, concretism:*** All over India, we experience the phenomenon of self-styled Gurus who promise remedies for each and everything. Adding to this dubious phenomenon, we have to face the fact that in Indian society, the people tend to believe almost everything, particularly if in disguise of some attire perceived as "holy". As a highly educated scientist told one of the authors: "Oh, I keep the *Puja* corner in our flat **just to be on the safe side**." At the same time, we know that so many "holy" persons are nothing else than crude business people who have the special talent of marketing themselves excellently. On this background, it is no wonder that traditional and modern *gurus* aplenty render their advices to all and sundry, and on top of that, they not only do very good

business but also, have a clout on influencing almost all areas of society.[1] If we take up the terms regionalism, ruralism, urbanism, we all know how powerful irrational, superstitious influences can be; the term "**concretism**", in the holistic approach, has to be set against irrationalism and superstitions and also, against other "isms" which confuse, muddy or more often clog an open-minded, realistic, future- and action-oriented view to the factual problems in our society.

3. ***From Government to Non-Government to Genuine Government:*** The term "Government" can be defined in so many different ways but here, should be defined in the Gandhian way as "Genuine" or, preferably, "non-governmental", like the authors interpret it.
   We have to ask: What is the very purpose of government? What parameters or organisational forms are implied in good governance? What is the role of bureaucracy in government? What is the role of politics in government? What is the cost of government? Who bears the cost of government? What are the tangible and non-tangible elements of government? What are the quantified and quantifiable factors of government? What are the qualified and qualifiable elements of government? Are there workable systems to question the powers?[2] Is government reduced to **wielding power to loot legally?**
   Is the government interested at all in answering these questions? If so, why is it not doing so? If not, why is that so?
   The authors are of the firm opinion: **Least governance is best governance.**
4. ***Role of professionals, from hobby to profession:*** The term "professional" seems to be used very often in a very non-professional manner, meaning that everybody who is able to convince somebody of the fact that he is doing anything at all is automatically "professional". We do not subscribe to this.
   Professionalism means that basic knowledge and skills are used to the utmost efficiency.
   Other chapters in this book show the respective roles and the importance professionals have to take up in holistic development set ups. In the present context, we like to put the finger

on the fact that issues like "efficiency" are closely connected with issues like "job satisfaction" and "developing hidden potentials", etc., so that we finally come to the ideal situation when genuine potential is used professionally, i.e. what we most like to do becomes our profession.

5. ***Re-defining excellence :*** Basically, nature in its totality shows us **excellence in action, transparent and sustainable.** As a holistic product of nature, human beings are capable of excelling provided the enabling environment is also excellent. We know that every human being is equipped with an individual packet of potentials and abilities (intellectual, psychological, and physical) which can be developed to its highest efficiency.
   In this book, it is not our purpose to elaborate about guidelines of operationalisation of excellence, but it is important, at the same time, explaining holistically issues which are closely related, like "excellence", "performance", etc., in the same system, to avoid any misunderstandings.
   We are of the opinion that it is not always possible to excel in one's activities, but the mindset of continuously **striving for excellence** is the decisive attitude which creates an environment where excellence at all levels can be achieved.
6. ***From Useless to Useful :*** We define the term "useless" as "used less", and, in the same way, "useful" as "used ful(ly)". The negative impact we perceive if the term "useless" is used, comes from the fact that there is hardly a more humiliating expression describing the abilities of a human being, meaning if somebody is "useless", then the person can be disposed off. We all have our individual USP[3], our own potential (see preceding para 5) which should be used fully.
   There is a proverb in Sanskrit, saying that there is nothing useless, because each herb has some medicinal property, each individual has some doing ability, and each word has some meaning, the only thing which is difficult to find is organizership.[4]
7. ***Operationalisation of best ideas :*** There is no shortage of so-called best ideas everywhere in India's world of knowledge and vision. The biggest problem is that of operationalisation, and this book is all about generating practicable ideas, models, systems and specific options for that purpose. It is an art, a

science, a practice, a mindset, where the best are differentiated from the worst and categorized as per the priorities of times and places.

The mindset of action-orientation is the basic prerequisite to achieve changes and/or developments at all. There can never be any rigid or fixed action-points which are static and could be practical for all people and situations, but a flexible outlook and the mindset for change.

8. ***Cost reduction, low-cost—high impact :*** To face the challenges of globalization effectively, it is imperative that all efforts are made in this direction. With better co-ordination, networking, planning and other efficient management methods, it is possible to have high impact—low cost systems at all levels. To achieve this, effective training, cost consciousness, and all round monitoring is a must.
9. ***Issues of frauds, conflicts and power :*** We are well aware that terms like "fraud" or "conflict" might be perceived totally different by people with very different vested interests. Generally, it is all about power, it use or its misuse. The lessons of history, development, rise and fall of civilization, leadership issues, when examined holistically, compel us to motivate the so-called commoners to understand the game of exploitation for which mainly "power" is (mis)used.

   Ultimately, it is behaviour like submissiveness, yielding to threats, conformism, opportunism, indifference, inability or unwillingness of acting according to one's cognition, which makes it so very easy to wield power and perpetually exploit the masses.

   If we go deeper into the perception of "fraud", we realize that this has become an almost normal attribute expected from everyone who is in a position of power at all levels. This attitude can only be changed by a change of mindset along Gandhian lines where "truth" has its strong meaning and civil disobedience is not perceived as something criminal. We know that "fraud" leads inevitably to "conflict". The latter can be solved, especially by methods and means taken up by courageous citizens who are conscious of their own, not yet realized power.
10. ***Recognize the unrecognized :*** In the schemes and systems of our developmental planning, it is sad that there are so many

completely neglected due to the fact that no recognition is taking place. These unrecognized have their own pride, place, position, value, rights, why then, are they unrecognized and most probably stay so? Does it mean that they are not worth to be recognized? What type of social mechanisms exclude them from the mainstream, from being recognized and given their due share in society?

What components have to go into a socio-political system which recognizes all of its members, namely the as yet unrecognized?

A society which thus excludes big parts of its population from being recognized in their own rights and dignity, giving them their fair share of the good of the country, cannot be considered fully civilized.

11. ***Need for networking*** : In view of the globalized and further rapidly globalizing economies, overall competition has become the key word. The weak, the dormants, the decentralized, the underprivileged, the dependents, have to ultimately network for their survival. The organized looters and exploiters already have their well-knitted networks, while those busy with their local surroundings did not react or act in time for different reasons. It is a pity that the established institutions, instead of facilitating efficient networking of underprivileged, on the contrary ruthlessly annihilated them.

    New future-oriented, holistic networking systems for all those who are not yet players in the global game, have to be introduced while international institutions are already convinced of these needs, but are still directionless or clueless as to what is to be done and how.

12. ***Back to the natural self, back to basics*** : In the speed of development allover the world, the basics of nature are often sidelined or completely neglected. Nature has its own systems of dying and creating as part of the circle of sustainability.

    Before it becomes too late, the imminent collapse of nature and its resources has to be fully realized and urgent steps have to be taken to enable future generations to live on this earth in humane conditions. Environment protection is only one part of this task, albeit one of the most important; but protection alone will not be enough, we have to actively restore natural surroundings by going back to our natural needs. As John Muir said: "When one tugs at a single thing in nature, he finds it attached to the rest of the world."

13. ***Determining work culture and work patterns :*** In operationalising processes of desired changes, this aspect of work culture and work patterns are often neglected. With the many diversities all around us and the individual nature of needs, aspirations, abilities, potentials, etc., work culture and with it work patterns vary greatly. Work success should be measured by achievements and not by static standards like it is done widely. Each leader will have to develop monitoring systems to bring out the best of all without diminishing the diversity. The term "job satisfaction" has to come into the focus of all concerned with work culture, as it enables enhancing of productivity, creativity and a healthy attitude towards everything concerning work performance.
14. ***Stakeholders, role players and experiences with capacities :*** A dynamic change agent, while operationalising change—whether difficult or simple—must keep in mind the experienced stakeholders and role players who have, most probably, capacities in action. Normally, only the organized are listened to and involved. Any change which is to be sustainable and equity-based must not neglect these groups but must actively involve them. They have to render basic and powerful support.
15. ***Women-facilitators of status quo?*** It is one of the very much tabooized issues to put the finger on the role of women in keeping up the development-hindering **status quo**. One the one side, the term "women's empowerment" is voiced everywhere, but in reality, it is vastly the women themselves who allow that they are instrumentalised to keep up the present state of condition.

For example :

- it is the women who bring up their male children with the same male-chauvinistic attitude as the husbands,
- it is the women who bring up their female children in the same submissiveness under which they are suffering,

- it is the women who submit themselves too willingly to the whims and wishes of their husbands,
- it is the women who yield to pressures from relatives, in-laws and husbands to procreate instead of following a career,
- it is the women who too willingly criticise their fellow-women when they are successfully following their opinions and missions,
- it is the women who too willingly give in to keeping up a façade towards society, even if they are suffering in their familiar situation,
- it is the women who do not exercise their human rights against perpetrators/violators, be it their own husbands, relatives or other persons.

As long as the women themselves do not realize their real power in changing the conditions in society, we cannot really hope for sustainable change. The majority of male persons in society cannot be counted upon as change agents as they are afraid of giving away their gender-related privileges and advantages. That means, not only have the women to realize their strength and exercise it, but the men have to emancipate and mature the same way. The aim and objective of this emancipatory process would be a healthy, egalitarian society.

REFERENCES

1. We know of many a politician who asks his personal guru for his astrology-based, or otherwise contrived, advice before taking a decision. There are innumerous, similar examples in the decision-making spheres in Indian society.
2. After all, we have a secular Democracy!
3. USP = Unique Selling Proposition, see Glossary.
4. "Amantra mantra nasti, nasti mul manoshadhaman, ayogya purusho nasti, yojaktrust durlabham". A few examples should be mentioned: Scientology, religious fundamentalists of all creeds, organisations which are instrumental in propagating racial issues, etc.

Chapter-11

ON POVERTY

It seems everybody has his own notion about poverty depending on the basic criteria and on the parameters applied.

Poverty in a global context, for example, is always dependent on the comparison of the given living standards in a respective society, the access to (consumer) goods, the level of education for everybody, health service infrastructure, and the like.

The perception of "poverty", be it individually defined or applied to certain strata of society, depends on the expectations of individuals or respective group members and has to be analysed from these angles.

In the so-called developed countries, i.e. highly industrialized, mostly Western world, the individual perception of being "poor" has completely different connotations from those in the so-called "under", or less developed countries. Individual living standards depend not only on the possible access to goods, education, development and secure living conditions, but also on the individual concept of life.

We observe that in the Western world, many people resort to a concept of "simple living", trying to shed all unnecessary luxuries, going back to "natural" living conditions which can make their practical day-to-day life quite miserable as the conditions in these countries make it more or less impossible to really live in tune with nature as here is hardly "nature" to be found to speak of. But this attitude, this concept of life has obviously nothing to do with the worldwide problem of poverty we are concerned with. "Voluntary Poverty" might be the right term for this, but it is nothing else than the pathetic try to turn the time back, defying the reality, trying to escape somehow. Especially pathetic is the sad combination of "Voluntary Poverty" with the artificially created conscience of solidarity with the starving masses in the world. It is very clear that such an attitude leads to stagnation as it lacks the essential element of action which would be necessary to turn a fictional solidarity into factual change.

Pseudo-academic standards want to make us believe that people in "under"-developed countries are satisfied with a concept of providing them with sufficient amount of food (measured in calories intake), clothing and shelter adjusted to climatic conditions. Per capita income is a similar useless criteria which does not help at all. It leads to the various help campaigns which we know are always too late, too less and too badly organized to really bring relief; also, what is even worse, it leads to permanent dependence on those campaigns, hindering sustainable change for self-reliance. Profiting from all these actions are the organizations themselves, worldwide do-gooders with their own vested interests.

Reliable and mostly applicable academic standards of research are used and published by the UN and World Bank, but these can be useful only if we take them as part of material to identify areas of urgent concern, or to compare vital statistic data to gain some overview on trends in development.

Usually, poverty is seldom defined by including the fields of education, the access to education and thus, further individual development.

Now, where can we go from here, where should be put the adjusting screw for bringing about change?

From the holistic angle, we have to take into account a bundle of influential factors determining the level of poverty and the needs of the people concerned which have to be tackled. Also, our approach has to be aim-oriented, meaning that parallel to all analytical efforts, all efforts cf understanding, defining, finding ways and means to reach those who need support in order to involve them as early as possible, the aim of creating conditions for self-reliance should always be integrated as the ultimate goal.

Since tremendous literature on poverty exists and all the governments since Independence have been laying stress on poverty removal without real success, we put only a few fundamental questions for better operationalization of human development:

1. What type of local resources, knowledge, skills, etc., are available within the community?
2. What are the reasons for their not being in practice and use?
3. Many areas of local security for the community like water, food, health, jobs, even funeral facilities, environment, law and order, overall quality of life, etc., need to be earmarked. Are there any local options and ideas? How can they be implemented and revived?

4. Based upon the lessons of the past, what problems of co-ordination, leadership, technology, financing, transport, infrastructure, language, even greed, etc. do they perceive?
5. How, with better leadership grooming and the use of IT, they could have better, transparent and observable preparedness and strategy for facing the disaster?
6. Can the policies of the Government re-enforce the capacity of the individuals and the community to ensure their own enhanced security? For example, can they develop, preserve and enhance the capacity of local godowns, local water storages, local health and herbs, etc., so that they have an interest in developing their capacity and their confidence?
7. Are there some models or communities which have done well in enhancing their capacity to fend for themselves? What lessons can be learnt with reference to policies of funding, training, monitoring, confidence building, etc., from them?

To sum up, we state and give the following suggestions :

1. The need for recognition, incentives and promotion has to be made a part of the competitive spirit building. It is here, with IT, that better transparent and bankable plans could be developed. This is an area of self-employment and better investment potentials. With bankable, viable and marketable propositions, it is possible to develop investment-oriented plan schemes. Banks, Government and the well-to-do of the society could provide viability-based incentives schemes and programmes. To elucidate, one could quote many examples such as providing loan for lakes and wells with payment and recovery-based incentives. In the same way, communities and villages could get incentives with better bankable schemes.
2. Issues of effective poverty preparedness and capacity as well as confidence building of the community are not different. Only those communities can fight disaster effectively who are prepared wholeheartedly and systematically. This means regular churning of issues and raising the levels of discussion.
3. The limitations of the government have to be properly appreciated. With the best of professionalism, issues of arbitrariness, ad-hocism, lack of transparency, corruption, nepotism, etc., cannot be left out. Ultimately, the local

institutions of governance and the community have to develop their capacity to face a multiplicity of challenges. Again, the harsh realisation of the fact that individuals and societies have to solve their own problems on their own needs to be effectively communicated.

4. The manual must also communicate through local language, pictures, case studies, instances and information, various dimensions of dependency, confidence building, proper planning, storages, and overall security. Creation of local cadres of volunteers from all communities and genders could go a long way in enhancing the capacity. In the same way, youth and women with expertise of the seniors and veterans could broaden the field of effective disaster management.
5. The manual must also involve the expertise and knowledge, normally not available with the local community. The Panchayati Raj Institutions are part of the constitutional structure. They need to be made effective partners of governance. This itself needs lobbying and proper placement in the budgetary and policy-making field of activities. In the West, lobbying and pressure building is a well developed subject of study and implementation. Those affected by disasters may not be able to lobby for themselves. But by broadening the issues of disaster and development, a viable proposition could be marketed. Issues of population, poverty, unemployment, malnutrition, girl child, old age, poor drinking water, poor health conditions, poor sanitation, neglect of animals and neglect of traditional knowledge and, on the whole, over-dependency from the State and from outside resources providers, etc., are much more serious. By neglecting the seriousness, long-term harm to peace, prosperity, harmony and the whole nature of civilization itself comes under serious questioning. The sustainable human development compels all of us to look into these poorly marketed areas of disaster with much more seriousness and concern.
6. The compartmentalized system of governance and policy-making further make the problem serious. Neglect of holistic churning of issues does not permit in totality the understanding and the nature of the problems. The constitutional and practical hope lies in the Panchayati Raj where many

subjects get converged. We hope that, with better leadership and better analytical ability of the trainers, cost effective, confidence building processes could emerge. It is very difficult, but efforts have to be made consistently in that direction.

7. The role of local teachers, community leaders, youth, senior citizens, spiritual institutions and, on the whole, of all those who have the urge and the skills to be of some use to the community needs to be canalized. As policies and the budgetary system encourage local capacity building, all these hidden investible potential power can be converted into a solid force and strength. Hence, the issues of proper policies and policing have to be studied. This can be done by institutions and NGOs, volunteers and contributors. The forum of holistic research analysis and action has to be formed and supported.
8. Under the former Chief Justice of India, Shri M. N. Venkatchalliah, a commission was formed to review the working of the Constitution. It has made some very important recommendations, both with regard to disaster management and Panchayats to be developed and declared as institutions of self-governance with exclusive functions assigned to them. The Commission had also brought out its concern very clearly in the following lines:

> "Even in the States which have shown political will to decentralise, devolution has not gone beyond entrusting to them responsibility for implementation of the schemes/projects conceived by the State or Union Government. As a result Panchayats have not blossomed into institutions of self-government. Instead they have been reduced to an implementing arm of the State Government."

Before we close, we do want to emphasize the need for analysing the specific terms "poor" and also, "poverty".

We are normally using the terms as, for example :

- poor speaker
- poor student
- poor eater

- poor performance
- poor writer
- poor trainer
- poor politician
- poor productivity
- poor sales
- poor results
- etc.,

all of which do not only mean money power but are referring to all sorts of deficiencies.

Now, when we shift from the term "poor" to the term "poverty", we find, for example,

- poverty of thoughts and ideas
- poverty of imagination
- poverty of views and clarity
- poverty of common sense
- etc.,

which has, obviously, completely different connotations. When it comes to poverty, there is the need to study the role of the Government of India, the State Governments, the local administrative and political bodies, the professional bodies, banks, the community-based institutions, the religion-based institutions, the NGOs, etc. Who is really determined to remove poverty, or who is able to remove poverty, or who will achieve the removal of poverty in the future?

We have to ask seriously if all those mentioned institutions are really interested in the removal of poverty. Logically, an institution which has its only aim and objective in removal of poverty would consequently lose its existence if it performs successfully. Can there be a serious commitment under these circumstances?

When we link up the above mentioned terms with the terms "prosperous" or "prosperity", as commonly used for example :

- prosperous people
- prosperous areas
- overall prosperous

- abundance
- affluence
- plenty
- resourceful
- etc.,

we have to re-define the relationship between these three terms, namely "**poor - poverty - prosperous**" to develop our non-conformistic strategy for development.

Poverty has synonyms in: beggary, destitution, neediness, pauperism, penury, want, etc., poor has synonyms in: unhealthy, ailing, debilitated, feeble, frail, ill, indisposed, infirm, invalid, sick, unsound, unwell, etc., while prosperity has synonyms in: fortune, affluence, bounty, luxury, money, opulence, plenty riches, success, wealth.

The above-mentioned synonyms have been intentionally incorporated here to highlight the urgent need for a differential, progressive, realistic, and holistic approach. It is a question of mindset of those who are planning, writing, thinking, and shedding crocodile's tears for the "poor" and because of "poverty". Has it not become a big business? Like those in the business of selling arms and ammunition all over the world while talking of peace, or else, like those propagating democracy while destroying it for the continuation of their hegemony in connection with big business?

Hence, first of all, we must recognize those areas and communities who have no poor or poverty-stricken people in their areas? We have to emphasize that "poor" in our holistic approach, does not mean "having nothing", which would reduce the meaning to material possessions. But, in reality, those "poor" have a lot of resources which they cannot put into good use, for example their brainpower, their creativity, and all their hitherto untapped potentials, which the nation is also deprived of.

Furthermore, the issue of globalization as poverty-reducing policy has been widely acclaimed, first of all by the World Bank. The "percolation theory" of the Government of India and the Planning Commission has miserably failed. In view of the urgency to find Implementable solutions, we must not neglect both these factors, i.e. globalization and the "percolation theory". We recommend the involvement of the people, the community, the Panchayati Raj, as the only solution to do away with this stigma.

We have to emphasize that in the holistic context, we deal with "poverty" in a completely different way; it is not something to be ashamed of but to **deal with**, it is not something to complain about, but to **deal with**, it is not something to keep under the carpet, but to **deal with**. In this spirit, many like-minded, committed people should join hands for actively generating hope in a sustainable way.

Chapter-12

Role and Problems of NGOs in Present Time

As the government's efficiency in solving the problems of the Indian society becomes less and less and has to be seriously questioned, another efficient delivery mechanism in this field has to be examined.

None of us would think of criticizing the role of NGOs in modern Indian history as they mostly tookover the hardest work in building up our modern society. It goes without saying that the government authorities at all levels would have disastrously failed without the work of NGOs.

It goes without saying that we do not go into the issue of fraud NGOs or other self-styled NGO-like dubious institutions. Those we leave to their fate.

We are convinced that sincere, hard-working NGOs have an important role to play in building up a more egalitarian society. But, at the same time, we feel it extremely important to place the index finger on the wounds of NGOs which have already started bleeding, to save them from extinction. This means that we are of the firm opinion that the NOGs have to change; not only change some of their activities or of their attitudes, but radically change their infrastructure and their outlook, becoming change agents themselves!

NGOs in the holistic sense have been in existence since long. With the globalization, economic liberalization, and, most important of all, the drastic reduction in the international help and funding budgets, most of the NGOs are now in a desperate situation. Having worked for about four decades with and around NGOs, and, having analyzed their contemporary problems, both the authors are speechless to find that in spite of various writings on the wall in the last two decades, there has been almost no shift towards self-reliance.

After our analysis, the main reasons for this debacle are the following:

1. Mindset and Attitudes

- Due to the fact that most NGOs are traditionally only focused on grants and subsidies, their mindset is thus determined. This prevented an early shift towards healthier economic set ups in time. We can say that this attitude is still prevalent, spoiling very often the ability to bring about change, even when rationally, the problem is well recognized.
- The above-mentioned mindset also has led to a lack of proper cost-consciousness which, in a type of vicious circle, led to inefficiency in organisational and personnel matters.

2. The first generation

- The generation of dedicated, visionary founders is now too senior to be actively involved in the running of the NGO, many of them are no more, or ill, or have given the reigns into other hands.
- Our analysis shows that an essential management imperative has not been taken up at all: creating an efficient second line leadership in time. This fact has led to the problem of various in-fights in institutions, lack of viable personal external contacts, lack of authority in decision-making, lack of foresight in the decision-making process, absence of future-orientation, absence of visions, fear of change.

3. Professionalism

- We noticed widely a **lack of professionalism** in running the institution, for different reasons:

  (a) wrong personnel decisions,
  (b) lack of organisational efficiency,
  (c) lack of management skills,
  (d) too much dependency on retired personnel,
  (e) lack of future-oriented decision-making,
  (f) lack of efficient networking and sharing experiences,
  (g) tendencies of sectarianism (isolating the institution).

- The founders are no more involved in the day-to-day activities; this means that their **visions**, rich experiences and their still important capacities are neglected and lost forever.

- No proper **documentation** of activities, successes and failures, has been systematically done. If a certain type of documentation has been carried out, it is mostly unsystematic or else, does only serve to show events with VIPs or some outstanding incidences or award ceremonies.
- **Cost control** or, what should be part of the mindset, cost consciousness, is reduced to a mere bureaucratic accountancy which leads to a static approach to finances, adverse to save money or to use it most cost-efficiently.
- **Retired Personnel:** The recruitment of retired personnel from all sorts of professions can be fruitful, provided they :

  → do not spend their time in the institution while their major interest is in getting additional salary,
  → do not hinder development by influencing the institution to further follow out-dated methods,
  → prevent the institution to recruit younger professionals who would better contribute to the development of the institution,
  → are not only employed because they are cheaply available while conveying out-dated values and methods.

4. Dependency on Grants and Subsidies

- As already mentioned above, the habit of relying on grants and subsidies has led to deplorable :

  (a) **Passivity** concerning striving for self-reliance,
  (b) **Passivity** through attitude of demanding support without making sure about delivering or proper performance.

- Cost-consciousness is almost nil in view of the previous experiences that somehow, support for projects is possible either from inside the country or from external donors.
- Activities and skills of personnel are wasted for conceptualizing projects aplenty to get grants and subsidies instead of using these resources for conceptualizing self-reliance.
- Conceptualizing project after project to keep day-to-day activities running has become a normal activity to circumvent the fact that many projects have a limited time in which they are subsidised, conceptualized with the aim to become self-reliant.

- No orientation on self-reliance due to focusing on donors.
- No formation of changing mindset within the institution towards self-reliance.
- Utter dependency on grants and subsidies creates very often foul compromises between donors and the institution in view of the necessities of the future.

5. Fear of change

- The basic question is: why was there no change in time when it had already become clear that outlook, infrastructure, set up of organisation, personnel (quantitative and qualitative), set up of external co-operation and contacts, etc., are no more sufficiently serving the requirements of current developments and, even more important, those of the future.
- In well-established institutions and/or communities, the fear of change is everywhere to be observed, albeit not all of the concerned people are really aware of it.
- It is a well-researched phenomenon that change, psychologically, is often perceived as threat, meaning threatening the well-established security, the safety of habits, the used-to-be, the secure feeling of "it has always been like this", even if the present conditions and the reality is miserable.
- Very often, an inherent lethargy, a status-quo-ism, cripples and paralyzes a whole institution, thus making efforts for change impossible.
- Another obstacle in the way of bringing about necessary change is the lack of compulsions, be it from inside the institution or induced from external sources, like donors or funding agencies. For example, proper control mechanisms and evaluation, accompanied by respective consequences, are very often not executed, thus leading to the attitude from the institution that they need not act at all.
- In these circumstances, the lack of distinct, sincere and business-like communication leads to an attitude of taking agreements not very serious; experiences show that in case of problems, the funding agencies/the donors would again come to help. In some NGOs, the art of artificially constructing difficulties concerning certain projects which are not properly taking shape, have become a speciality.
- In all, we observed a number of unfortunate attitudes and

atmospheres in which younger people do not find the right climate for perspectives in life and career. They do not get proper training for developing their abilities and skills, they cannot realize their creative ideas and the best of them are either compelled to leave the institution altogether or somehow manage to stick along, and draw their salary in frustration.

The same way, young people get depressed when they feel the lack of genuine conviction and action-oriented approach within the institution. This is often due to the fact that because of financial constraints, too many retired people, very often retired bureaucrats, are employed which has five main disadvantages:

(a) they block positions for young people,
(b) they stand in the way of innovations,
(c) they continue with their stereotyped practices,
(d) they are in positions where they determine the functioning,
(e) they are opposed to change.

6. **Aims and Objectives**

In the many decades of their existence, most of the NGOs lost their clear orientation on the aims and objectives for which they were founded. Due to the day-to-day struggles, the many obstacles they had to overcome, the manifold activities which happened to come in their way, etc., led to an almost directionless reacting to the day-to-day needs and/or demands. Now, we notice a widespread lack of clear aims and objectives. This adds to the overall inefficiency in organization and infrastructure.

What is to be done?

The authors do not assume to provide answers to all the burning problems in society, but they are of the firm opinion that most of the current problems could be solved with the right mindset and the necessary determination. This, of course, concerns a very vital nerve of the existing NGOs, namely the efficiency of the decision-making processes.

If a **holistic** turnkey-consultancy is agreed upon, it is of utmost importance that the reorganisational process is requisitioned with the necessary executive powers as otherwise, the whole exercise will be completely futile. It can mean, of course, implementing hurtful personnel decisions, it can lead to turning the institution upside down, it can lead to a radical change of orientation, of aims and objectives, it can lead to severing contacts and ties to hitherto normal contacts, etc.

Generally, there cannot be a doubt that **radical change** is needed to solve the problems of the NGOs. Now, "change" is exactly the turning point of all ventures, of all suggestions and of all solutions.

The authors are well aware of the fact that nothing in this world is so easy to talk about and hardly nothing as difficult to practice than **change**. It starts with our own habits which are so immensely difficult to change even if we are very consciously working on it. How difficult it is then for groups of people to change, how difficult it is for leaders to convince people to change, how difficult it is for institutions to bring about change within their accustomed habits.

The basic hindrance for change is fear, as we mentioned above. People do not want change because they are afraid of losing their accustomed safety, even if it is very uncomfortable for them, even if it is exploiting them, even if they are well aware that they are suffering and that things could be improved. Why is that so?

Psychology tells us that human beings are normally afraid of change for fear that things could become worse. They are afraid of losing their comparatively safe or secure surroundings. **Habits** become the safe harbour where even uncomfortable, adverse or even hostile conditions are accepted or adjusted to, as long as there is no change. We do not venture in psychological reasoning, but we do subscribe to these findings: why else should human beings submit to conditions they clearly perceive as hostile to them? Why else should human beings consent to conditions which are clearly not in tune with their own aims and objectives? Why else should human beings remain in conditions they know are not leading to their goals?

Because they are afraid of change. This being frightened leads them to accept adverse conditions even if they know how to bring about change. It is one of the unsolved riddles in human behaviour.

Generally, the same applies to all institutions as we analysed the NOGs. Of course, in NGOs, we detect different bundles of reasons for detesting change, but basically, the atavistic fear of change overrules everything.

These aspects have never been seriously discussed so far, as probably the right time had not set in. In the meantime, all are now suffering from these main blows and we will put the finger in the wounds:

1. **Reduction in grants and subsidies**
   The fact that there will be drastic reductions in grants and subsidies from all funding agencies, governmental or non-governmental, national or international, and also, from private donors, has been well known since the last two decades. Like the ostrich who puts its head into the sand, most of the NGOs just did the same.

2. **Competition**
   After realizing the fact that the above-mentioned fund reduction has already massively started and affected their functioning, the NGOs now are amidst a fierce fight for funds. This has led to very unfortunate situations: some NGOs stopped long-established co-operations for fear of having to share donations, well functioning information channels have been severed, and even the exchange of know-how and skills has been stopped. Thus, decade-old loyalties and chains of informal mutual support have stopped to exist, to the disadvantage of all.

3. **Globalization**
   To face the challenges of globalization, NGOs have to restructure and reposition themselves. The international funding institutions are expecting changes in the attitudes but most of the NGOs do not know how to go about it. This is, at the same time, a blow and a challenge, a curse and a blessing.

4. **Governmental institutions**
   In the last two decades, many State governments have established their own NGOs which either belong to political parties or government departments, and they are headed by bureaucrats or politicians. This has been done to facilitate additional funding provided by international bodies, the governments and the politicians wanted to have their own big piece of the cake and use the bounty for their own vested interests. This too, has been a blow and a challenge to the traditional NGOs.

5. **Personnel problems in NGOs**
As mentioned above, there are various problems concerning personnel within NGOs: the shift from one generation to the other has not been smooth and harmonious, let aside planned or well organized. The fact that almost all the so called founding fathers were of very impressive and sometimes overwhelmingly charismatic personalities, led to the well known consequence that within their circle of influence, hardly strong personalities could develop. In India, we all know that under the Banyan tree no other plants can flourish. Adding to this, the founding fathers missed to intentionally build up a second line leadership. All the NGOs have now to face the problem that no strong personalities are available to lead the institutions into a bright future.

In the following, we will give suggestions and advice, models and ideas for solving these problems. In this spirit, we are gladly offering to facilitate in the practical implementation process if required.

Understanding basic NGO facilitators

Since NGOs do not operate in isolation, we have to have a multi-pronged strategy by involving and identifying the role of the following:

1. **Planning Commission** : with its Voluntary Action Cell can do a lot in terms of policies, funding systems and monitoring.
2. **International bodies like World, Bank, UNDP, ILO, DFID, EU,** etc., with their vast network of planning, funding, training NGOs, and their financial powers could make a lot of difference in changing the mindset of NGOs. We agree with the many that are of the opinion that these bodies do not strive hard enough to change the mindset of the NGOs to be self-reliant and to improve their overall performance. This lead to the already mentioned attitude of the NGOs to take all the programmes and schemes for granted without really having to deliver results themselves.
3. **The Finance Ministry, Bankers, NABARD, CAPART, and similar authorities and bodies,** with their generous manning by All India Service civil servants, hardly adopt new approaches and in fact do the same mistakes in doling out

the scarce resources of the taxpayers while not putting emphasis on demanding results from the NGOs and, at the same time, do not even exercise proper accountability. The problem of lack of coordination between these authorities is already dealt with above.

4. **Federation of NGOs, trustees, and chartered accountants,** with their closest insight of the functioning of the NGOs, should be professionally committed to improve their performance.
5. **The importance of grading and/or self-grading of NGOs,** with its overall healthy consequences, would bring about clarity and propensity for self-improvement. NGOs could also be categorized in different sectors like

   - pure charity
   - semi-charity
   - semi-commercial
   - commercial.

   By properly charging the customers and/or the people served, and with a better and efficient management, the grading of NGOs would automatically improve, thus enabling them to realize their full potentials.

The International Institute for Holistic Research and Voluntary Action (Germany and India) has taken upon itself the task of helping those who want to help themselves and is committed to a holistic approach on modern Gandhian lines to face the challenges of globalization and help bringing about peace.

The help for NGOs and all institutions can be rendered through training, case studies, HRD, performance evaluation and analyses, bridging gaps, planning to market the unmarketed, documentation, policy options, developing quality standards, developing success parameters, sharing international experiences in environment protection and enhancing productivity, etc.

Chapter-13

Networking/Co-operation and Turnkey Consultancy

The necessity of networking both, in the country and also, globally, is of essential importance, especially when we stress on a holistic approach.

The reasons are obvious:

- achieving more efficiency by exchanging view and experiences (avoiding same mistakes);
- saving time and money by emulating already practised methods/models of development;
- supporting valuable experiments by innovative partnerships;
- enriching each other by personal contacts;
- enabling partners to work for better international understanding and world peace;
- building up ties with NRIs (which could result in getting them engaged in India's rural development);
- open up financial support.

It goes without saying that international co-operation should be carefully scrutinized in view of reliability, involvement in certain—political, religious, or otherwise—activities in their respective home countries[1], as these should be in tune with our aims and objectives.

International co-operation should be in the interests of all; especially in our context, where we cannot recommend charity partners, as this would again lead to inactivity, craving for funds and grants.

International charitable organisations play an important role in funding NGOs, no doubt about it, but in view of instigating entrepreneurship, self-initiative, such direct co-operations would be contra-productive. Of course, the exchange of ideas and experiences should be extended to these organisations, too. Those who are doing useful work will have lots of practical experiences which they can share to the advantage of all who are interested in eradication of poverty, global understanding and peace. To attain this, international seminars and workshops play the most important role.

Fruitful co-operation can evolve with the upcoming "Social Entrepreneurs"; mainly we can describe this laudable commitment of private companies as an openly declared attitude to take into consideration not only the interests of shareholders and profit-making but also the well-being and uplift of those who need it. This is a very big step towards holistic orientation, albeit still a long way to go.

In short, networking should lead to

→ Simplifying activities
→ Systematizing and Structuring plans
→ Speeding up activities
→ Sharing experiences
→ Enriching partners
→ Save time, money and energies

Since networking, co-operation and turnkey-consultancy are inseparable form each other, we ask some important questions like

- Who will network?
- Why should they be networked?
- With whom networking should be avoided?
- What are the issues in sustaining or breaking up the vicious circles and their permanent stakeholders who will not permit any operationalization of good ideas?
- Which are the areas of saturation and fighting for survival where networking is helpful?
- What will be the system of prioritization?
- Who will provide wings to thoughts and facilitate flying?

Without being too philosophical[2] the authors want to highlight some issues of profit, gain, benefit, fame, name, prestige, recognition, ego, hierarchy, status, greed, truth, wholesome, natural. In this book, the philosophy behind vital issues is not elaborated, nor are the psychological facets of many behavioural phenomena and of group behaviour explained in depth. This is not the intention of this book. The authors will go deeper into some of the important issues to be explained in one of the next issues of this series of books on holistic development.

Turnkey Consultancy

Much has been elaborately said and written about Turnkey Consultancy, especially by those who might have theoretical knowledge about models of how to achieve goals in development projects, but are lacking the necessary competence which can only be achieved by going to the grassroot level, involving the people concerned, taking into consideration the holistic outlook.

The term has become most fashionable; we all know that a good cause, when becoming fashionable, will be in danger of being reduced to superficial actionism catering to all those who have mainly in mind to fill their own pockets.

On this background, scrutinizing thoroughly all those who offer Turnkey Consultancy is of utmost importance.

It is necessary to define the term "consultancy" in the holistic context and also, specify the fields of action which should be covered by consultants, provided they fulfil our criteria of sincere code of conduct, i.e. "good governance".

Consultancy has to be done professionally: the role of professionals cannot be covered by the term "experts" as it most probably will not include our demand for holistic approach. Of course, expertise in respective fields are basic requirements for good consultancy, but at the same time, it cannot stop at this.

Turnkey consultancy in its proper concept, is a valuable instrument in the set up of holistic models of action, as it provides overview of all aspects of a given plan or project and, at the same time, ensures that delay in projects will be avoided, proper systems development is ensured by evolving a suitable infrastructure and, that core competencies are identified and put into place.

In the era of globalization, governments are unable to provide competitive services at the right time. Hence, a cadre of Self Employed Change Agents as Turnkey Consultants can facilitate problem solving.

We offer the following suggestions for better, efficient servicing mechanisms:

→ All the NGOs, training institutions, local governments, must create a cadre by giving them adequate training and incentives.

→ Rewards and returns for organizing successful cadres need to be given policy support.

→ Women and women's organisations can be very important facilitators.

→ NRIs and foreign funders should be provided special policy packages for awakening villages.

→ Senior citizens and retired persons, if not driven by mere greed and, not adverse to change, can be very important facilitators.

→ Vocational education institutions must train their trainers to provide turnkey consultancies so that they have practical experience and also, earn for the institute.

→ More and more policy support with liberalization should be offered to private entrepreneurs.

→ The mind-boggling problems of liberalization, globalization, poverty and over-population with the utter insensitivity of the governments, can be effectively tackled only by creative cadres of turnkey consultants.

→ The International Institute for Holistic Research and Voluntary Action is committed to provide training, turnkey consultancy with monitoring services at affordable costs to various bodies of self-governance, federations, NGOs, and Government departments. All can contact this Institute by *e-mail: intinst2006@aol.com;* it has also offered to provide franchise to all those who have commitment to holistic development by providing suitable packages of training to trainers, case studies evaluation and also opportunities to gain practical experiences on national and international level through direct connectivity with like-minded, dedicated experts.

REFERENCES

1. A few examples should be mentioned : Scientology, religious fundamentalists of all creeds, organisations which are instrumental in propagating racial issues. etc.
2. The authors feel it important to mention the real meaning of "philosopher", as they observed a heinous misunderstanding of the term. The greek word "Philosophos" merely refers to one who loves knowledge. One of the finest philosophers of modern times, Bertrand Russell, said:
   1. "Thought is subversive and revolutionary, destructive and terrible, thought is merciless to privilege, established institutions and comfortable habit. Thought is great and swift and free."
   2. "The whole problem with the world is that fools and fanatics are always so certain of themselves and wiser people so full of doubts."
   3. "Do not fear to be eccentric in opinion, for every opinion now accepted was once eccentric".
   4. "It has been said that man is a rational animal. All my life I have been searching for evidence which could support this."

Chapter-14

VILLAGE CHANGE AGENT
(WITH HOLISTIC APPROACH)

In the process of operationalization of change, especially in the rural context, the experience of bringing about change by government functionaries has been disastrous. It is a pity that these supposed-to-be change agents never lived up to the professional expectations. Now, they act only as grant-rebate-subsidy-quota-permit-licence—distributors, in short: they have become exploiters as power-wielding bureaucrats. They never defined their role as facilitator of change for development.

For this main reason, the authors suggest to establish a completely new holistic setup, driven by the spirit of self-initiative and private entrepreneurship, starting with the "**Self Employed Village Change Agent", SECA**.

In the context of holistic, practice-oriented approach for enhancing productivity and self-employment in villages, the self-employed "**Change Agent**" can be of great value to facilitate and support new ventures. He can be instrumental in bringing about attitudes of hope and self-initiative.

The following defines the term and describes the main roles a Village Change Agent should play:

> The Change Agent is an important opinion leader, motivator and coordinator, a mediator between conservatism and modernism, between the organised and the unorganised. He has his own thrust on self-employment and serves as role model for self-initiatives as a self-enlightened professional.
>
> He is part of the village society, he talks to the people, he lives with them, he knows them and their needs, and he earns his livelihood by serving them.
>
> He has to be given all support by the local authorities and by all established enterprises and opinion-leaders. It is our firm

conviction that the SECA could become a model for rural leadership in the future. With the 29 subjects[1] earmarked in the Constitution of India as responsibilities of the grassroot bodies, mainly Panchayati Raj, he is supplied with a solid fundament for his activities.

Defining the functioning, the special role of the Change Agent in a holistic set up, is necessary to show the crucial tasks he has to take up; a Change Agent is generally somebody who instigates changes in a given set up where changes are necessary to achieve a certain goal.

Practical steps

Example : Identifying a suitable Village "Self Employed Change Agent"[2] (SECA). This model for self-employment and, at the same time, enhancing productivity in villages, was designed by one of the authors, Dr. Taori, and has been already put into practice in some pilot localities.

1. Fixing characteristics (**work ability profile**); in this case the person should have :

    - good communication abilities,
    - good negotiating skills,
    - appreciation in the community,
    - adequate education,
    - decent lifestyle.

2. With these characteristics, suitable persons can be identified through :

    - local bodies like village Panchayat,
    - local self-help groups,
    - local individuals,
    - public information's: these will, at the same time, serve as **village information forum** about the scheme, later on helping in involving people.

3. From these first two steps, a number of persons will come forward, interested in the work. After pre-selection in view of the (1) mentioned characteristics, a workshop[3] should be conducted which should give additional information about :

- self-esteem, self-confidence,
- creativity and flexibility,
- attitude to work,
- self-initiative.

4. The results form the workshop will reduce the number of eligible persons to a few only. With these, single interviews[4] are to be conducted.
5. By comparing the results, the decision-making is very easy and enables, within the normal quota of errors which is inherent in all decisions concerning personnel, to do justice to all candidates:

   - Immediate positive decision for a certain person,
   - basis for discussing strengths and weaknesses with all the candidates which will help them in the future to concentrate on work more suited for them.

Evaluation Tool I
Example: General Suitability Profile as SECA

Criteria to be assessed	*Ideal Work Profile*				
	1	2	3	4	5
Communication skills					x
Negotiation skills					x
Appreciation/status in community					x
Education (i.e. graduate)					x
Adequate lifestyle and behavioural patterns					x

Note : Criteria have to be adjusted to the SECA work profile.

Individual Candidate's Profile

Criteria to be assessed	*Ideal Work Profile*				
	1	2	3	4	5
Communication skills					
Negotiation skills					
Appreciation/status in community					
Education (i.e. graduate)					
Adequate lifestyle and behavioural patterns					

Legend: Criteria have to be assessed: 1 = not assessed, 5 = highly assessed.

Easy handling: The "Ideal work profile" is to be compared with the actually assessed profile of the candidate—the suitability is asserted in no time. More so, it can be easily decided if weak spots can be improved, what is to be done in this case, when should this be done, what institution can cater to that.
Immediately, you have the "qualification measures" fixed and the plan is already finalised.
Also, if weak point cannot be improved, it is a valuable instrument for decision-making, and for transparency in explaining it to the respective candidate.

Advantages of this systematized method of selection

- clear view on necessary abilities
- time-saving
- easy to organise
- comparable results providing high safety in decision-making
- transparency of decision-making
- useful for all candidates who gain through objective information about their strengths and weaknesses (personality development)
- further qualification measures are automatically given (from comparing work ability profile with ability profile of the candidate)
- applicable to all other sorts of work profiles.

Training measures for SECAs

As mentioned above, the comparison of work ability profile with individual ability profile renders **automatically** the necessary training measures which will enable the candidate for the job[5], as it shows clearly the probable deficiencies in the "individual profile" compared with the "ideal profile".

Institutions and/or agencies which intend to take up this self-employment scheme "SECA" have to make sure that the necessary training facilities are available. Either they are in a position to provide the necessary training themselves, or they find the right institution and advise the SECA accordingly. At the same time, the future SECA should be prepared to pay for the training. The same as he will be paid for his services later on.

Training programmes for SECAs should be carefully planned according to the already existing abilities, skills, strengths and weaknesses of the individual. By applying the above shown method, we already know about eventual deficiencies or weak points in view of excellent performance, thus we just take these up and put it into practice.

For this, a training programme consisting of **modules** is to be set up; it will be highly flexible and enables to use only those modules which are really necessary. The "**Module System**" is systematic, time-saving and very efficient.

Why should somebody go through trainings which he does not really require? Be it that he is already equipped with the respective knowledge or skills or else, or be it that due to specific local conditions certain modules are obsolete.

An example for the **Module Method** is given below:

The required modules for the SECA's training programme should, shown in a simplified form, contain the following:

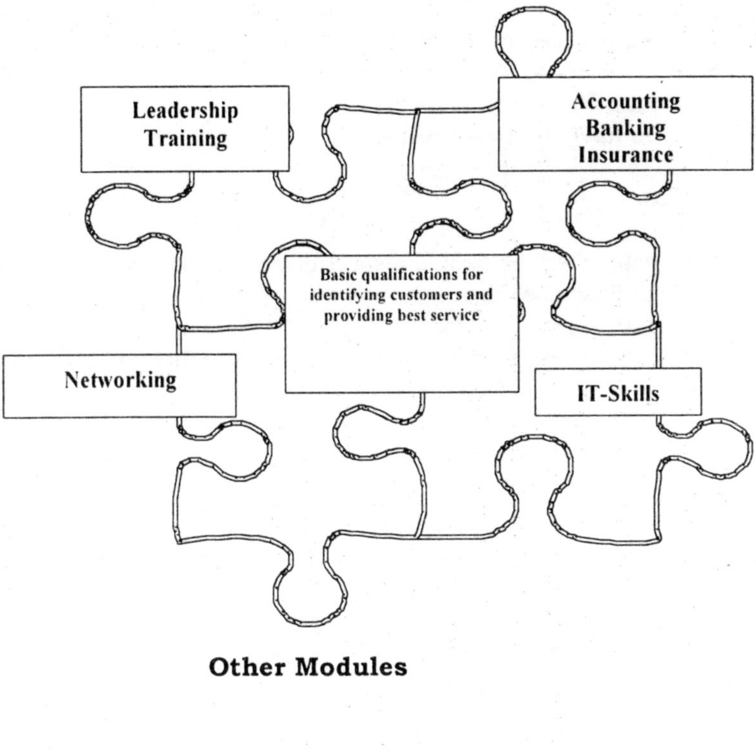

Local conditions may require additional knowledge and/or skills; these respective modules can be easily put in. Those locally required knowledge/skills have to be identified mainly through experience, through being acquainted with all conditions and problems in a given village; and the fact that they can be necessary requirement should be taken into consideration from the beginning.

The Module System of a training programme also has the advantage of supporting the respective modules in different institutions without breaking the system.

Village approaches

How should the SECA proceed to pursue his tasks efficiently? What practical steps can be suggested? Which methods should be applied to perform efficiently?

He should, as a first step, carefully prepare a convincing "SECA-Programme" which should explain clearly what he has to offer. He has to efficiently market himself, establish trust, confidence and make it clear, that he has to offer valuable service, as contrary to be a "servant".

There is a German proverb: **"If you want that others pay respect to you, you have to invoke respect."**

It means :

(a) that we will be treated respectfully only when we ourselves have genuine self-respect and when we show respect to others, and
(b) that we have to shed submissiveness, servility and giving in to demands which are not in tune with our aims, our ways and means, in short: we must not allow others to determine our own performance.

The SECA has to approach people self-confidently, convinced about his mission. He has to decide about the first practical steps as they might determine his success or his failure; in his village, he has a variety of possibilities, namely approaching all formally or informally organised groups and single persons.

The following shows the overall fields of activities of a Village SECA:

Within the Village :

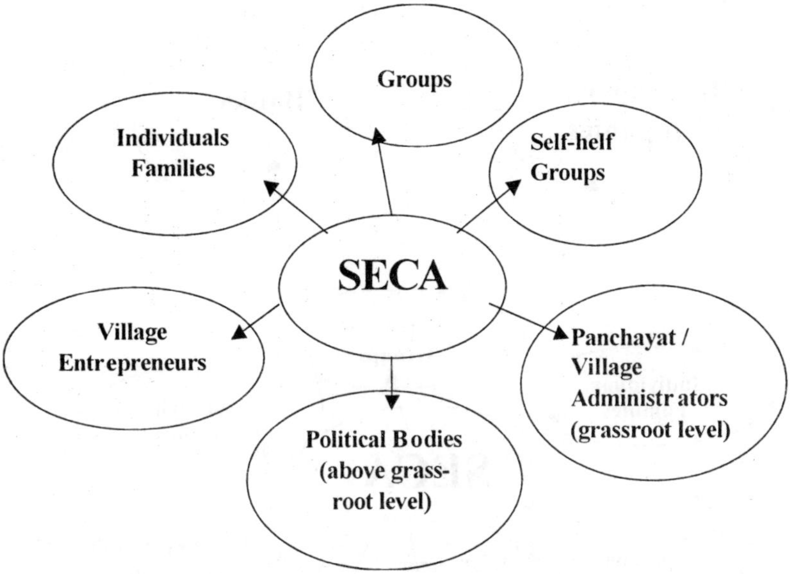

He has to be careful to avoid being instrumentalised by political vested interests, as he must not get involved in village groupism, thus antagonising parts of his prospective customers. One of the great advantages in approaching groups is the fact that he reaches several persons in one go and also, that he will have to deal with more than one opinion at one time. The effect of multiplying his information is also much more effective than while dealing with single persons, not to forget the effect of mouth-propaganda.

The village SECA should live and behave like a fish in the water with other fishes around; united against those who are exploiting their surroundings, depriving them of their essentials for a self-sustained, dignified life, united against the big fishes trying to swallow them up.

His role as facilitator could grow into a broader task: that of a mediator in case differences have to be sorted out, (small) problems between neighbours, families, village authorities, etc., can be tackled and solved this way.

Approaches outside the Village :

External contacts and co-operation

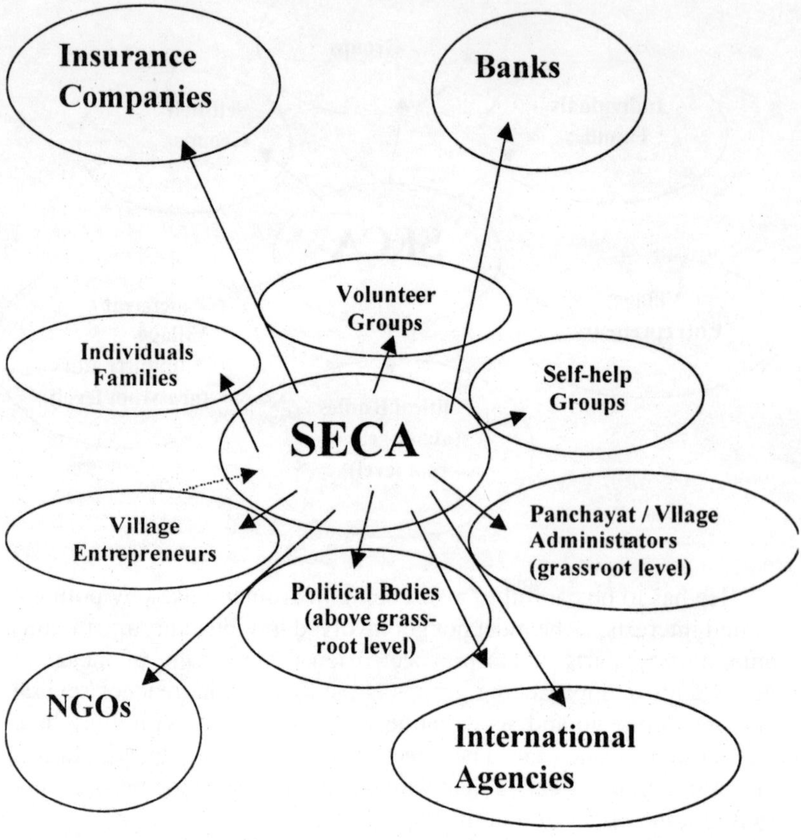

Practical example for Self-Employment

"Service Packets"— Pooling Knowledge and Skills

An example for village self-employment is the idea of offering services in a "turnkey way", i.e. all service or work to be done is taken over completetely, even if different skills and/or artisanship are required. Customers will be relieved from

- searching for the different experts
- coordinating timings
- checking (overall) costs

to name the only the most important advantages of the "Service-Packet-System".

This system is already well established in the West and can easily be adjusted to conditions in India. The target groups will mainly be the middle and upper classes who can afford to buy services. They are interested in having the necessary work done in a convenient way, as they only have to deal with a single competent person and at the same time, will be given a fixed overall prize.

It provides, cost-wise and time-wise, more security for the customers and is not identical with the "contractor"-system which is prevalent in India in this context, as according to all experiences, we know that it is extremely difficult to get compensation when things go wrong. The contractor will always refuse to takeover the responsibility for flaws and shift it to the sub-contractors whom the customer might not be able to take to task or sometimes even trace them. In any case, filing complaints with the courts seems futile and also, it would take too much time to get any result.

With the "Service-Packet-System", the customer can feel much safer provided the person responsible is performing well, of course. But, in the context of village conditions, a bad-performing or a non-performing Service-Packet provider will only survive with his business if he is performing well as everybody will come to know immediately. So, the quality of performance is the most important marketing instrument.

The Service-Packet-Provider establishes his own private company.

The Service-Packet-System can be organised in two different forms:

1. Single enterprise with affiliated experts
2. Collective enterprise

which are shown below with the means of example.

Example : **"Plumbing services":**

1. Single Person Private Enterprise

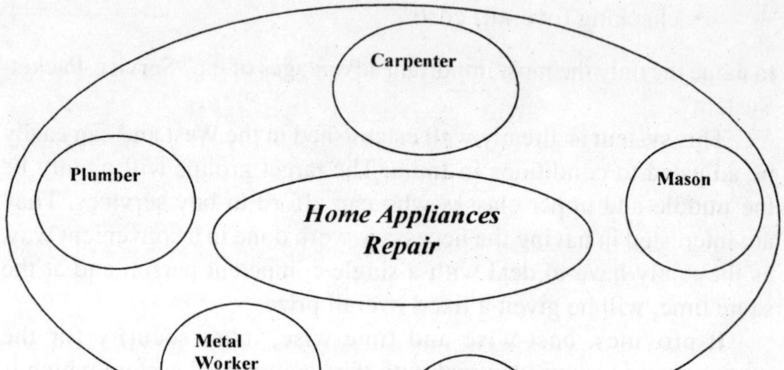

2. Collective Private Enterprise

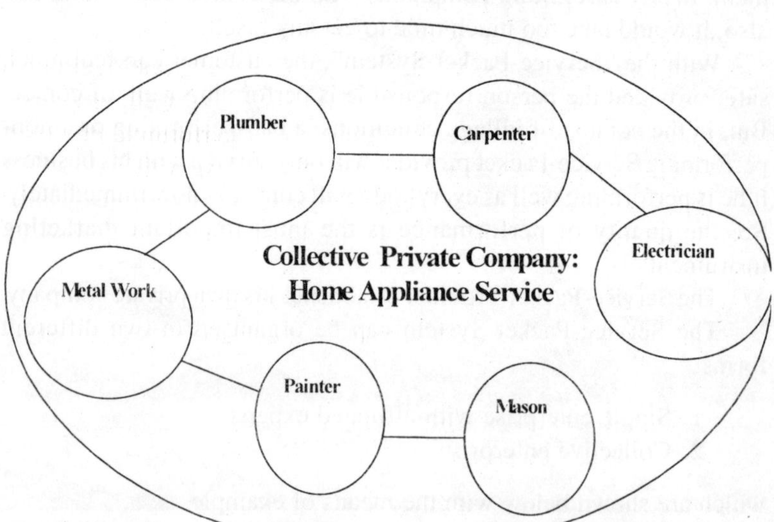

From these graphs we can broadly see the design of the system; according to the specific situation, the village entrepreneurs have to decide about the type of private company which is to be set up.

> **Description 1 :** Here, the Company is owned by a single entrepreneur only, affiliating related professionals/experts with it. The affiliation should be termed in a way that the entrepreneur can count on their services at any time required; this should be agreed upon in written form so that the organisational work does not suffer. At the same time, the affiliated artisans be free to follow their own businesses, they can take orders independently from the Service Company, provided the timings are not contradictory to the company plan and are agreed upon with the company. The commitment to the company should have utmost priority so that its reliability does not suffer.
>
> **Description 2 :** Here, the Company is established and owned by a group of several professionals/artisans who run the business. They will take mutual decisions and accept one among them as manager who is responsible for all organisational work, for the design of a single order, for supervising, for marketing the company and also, for the direct contact with the customers. Ideally, the owners of the company should concentrate on the running of the company and share tasks which might not exactly fit into the framework of their respective professions, thus they can show their entrepreneurial attitudes and skills.

Variant: Others can be affiliated, too, like in these will be professions which are seldom required. With those, the company will also agree on the—infrequent—affiliation in written form. It goes without saying that the management of the company has to first make sure that the affiliated professionals are available during the required time span, before a binding contract with the customer is designed and agreed upon.

Monitoring

Many valuable development projects became failures because no follow-up measures were implemented to ensure success and sustainability; in many cases follow-up plans were not even intended! Especially in the first phases of the running of a scheme, proper monitoring is a must!

If this precondition is established, there will be much greater security of achieving success, as :

1. a lot of clarity enters initial stages of a project due to the fact that concrete measures of monitoring the development show strength and weaknesses of it and also, the feasibility of the concept,
2. proper monitoring has to **be an integral** part of the scheme,
3. monitoring has to be fixed as a transparent system of **milestones** connected with definite timings,
4. the method of monitoring has to be clearly defined and agreed upon by all participants and those concerned,
5. if possible, the milestones should be connected with scenarios of "What to do when" (meaning what is to be done when a certain problem crops up by already describing the possible solution or steps to be taken).

Now, monitoring seems to be somehow confused with lots of additional work, whereas in reality, provided it is systematically planned as integral part of a scheme, it actually relieves from the workload. As with everything which is dependent on good organisational patterns, we have to make sure that responsibilities are clearly assigned and the person is qualified for the job.

A German proverb in management circles says: **"Where there are two or more people made responsible, nobody feels responsibility."**

All experiences, be it in private enterprises, be it in the highly bureaucratized set ups of government offices, we find the practical prove: wherever the responsibilities are not clearly defined and connected to proper decision making processes, the performance suffers and productivity goes down.

With the following **Milestone System** we achieve several goals at one time, especially processes like:

- clarity, transparency
- confidence-building
- efficiency

- enhancing productivity
- systematization
- in-time intervention possibilities.

If we take again the example of the village SECA, we can illustrate it like in the following (simplified) steps:

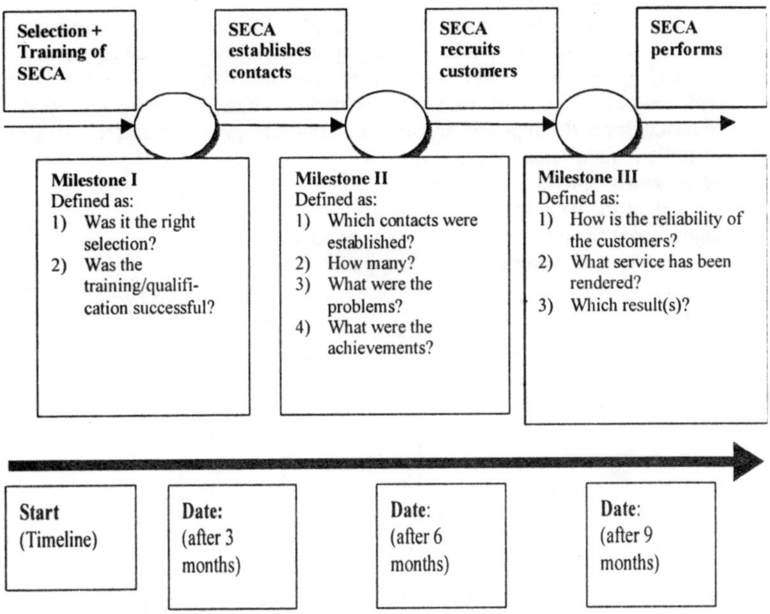

Milestones have to be defined as **checkpoints** by exactly describing the **aim and/or fact** which is to be reached/stated at a given time. At the same time, the definitions of the milestones should be restricted to the most crucial aims or facts to avoid the danger of bureaucratization lurking on every corner. It should be clear, upfront, as simple as possible, and understandable for everybody.

Furthermore, this method helps to enhance **clarity** in thinking and also, forces to think in an **aim-oriented manner**. If the SECA is well trained, he himself is responsible for the work processes. Every milestone he reaches successfully in time will enhance his self-confidence, and thus his self-motivation.

Last but not least, it goes without saying that the SECA is to be involved in the milestones plan from the start, be it with the definition of the aims, or be it with the time-fixing. After some experiences and also, after some success in fulfilling milestones, the SECA will be well equipped with self-confidence and the necessary skills to design his programmes and plans accordingly.

REFERENCES

1. 73rd and 74th Amendments to the Constitution has earmarked a number of subjects to be handled by local bodies. In the absence of suitable expertise and staff, these tasks which were earlier performed by State government employees, have to be performed by local bodies. The SECA cadre, if properly organised, trained, supported and utilized, can be a very important instrument as a holistic facilitator for development.
2. See appendix, glossary.
3. Contents of the workshop: see appendix.
4. Standardized form for interview: see appendix.
5. See also form "training measures", appendex.

Chapter-15

THE CHALLENGE OF OUR TIME

(MANAGEMENT IN THE RURAL CONTEXT - GLOBAL VISION AND LOCAL ACTION)

In the rural context, we feel that **management** has to be re-defined, specifically oriented on the organisational tasks to be fulfilled and also on sustainable models for self-employment and enhancing productivity, including solving financial problems and dealing with bureaucratic obstacles.

As already mentioned before, the time has come when rural management in the context of globalization receives the attention it deserves. By paying attention through compartmentalized approach, a lot of harm has already been done. Mass suicide by farmers in various pockets of India precisely bring out the need for a holistic approach. It is also a fact that due to lack of coordination, scarce resources of the Government are being squandered away which results ultimately in deepening the gap between the people and the government. Hence, low-cost, sustainable holistic systems need to be developed and implemented by paying attention to the following :

- Research and development in decentralised sectors
- From government to non-government to genuine government
- Gurus and context of regionalism, ruralism, urbanism, concretism
- Developing and replicating effective models
- Involving all existing resource-holders to diversify and reach out to the people
- Shifting practices to organic and locally re-cyclable type of systems development
- Involving cluster-based developmental initiatives with banks, entrepreneurs and marketing-driven investment consultants
- It is imperative that in the process of marketing the unmarketed, all unused or under-used infrastructure, skills, knowledge,

technologies, are identified and fully use, preferably on Public-Private-Panchayat Partnership.

While global vision and local action requires a holistic understanding and the developing of a plan of action, it is not as simple as that. It will require leaders and consultants of really high vision and ability for implementation.

The main problem lies in the internal resource generation by institutions which have been hitherto conditioned on "grant mindset". Hence, the turnkey consultants, the change agents, policy makers and all others in the field have to accept the need for massive changes all around. We hope, many more institutions and individuals would come forward and take up the challenges of change in the globalized economy by networking and strengthening the grassroots.

Marketing-led Operationalisation of Sustainable Development

In the last century, development has been unsustainable and also, grant/charity-driven. The time has come when the weaknesses of these practices have been well recognized and also, the enormous harm done has been widely recognized. Despite this, there is the problem of finding a suitable strategy and the tactics for correcting this widespread misconception.

As already mentioned, the real damage lies in the overall "dependency syndrome" which has overpowered the society. The influence of the government has been crippled by its inability to provide adequate grants to all the claimants. **The soft nature of the State gets further punctured due to organized lobbies that corner the scarce resources.**

All these ultimately scare away self-employment and entrepreneurship resulting in forcing the common man to look for State grants. Ultimately, this results in chaos and finally in disaster.

Marketing-led development precisely tries to tackle these issues effectively by laying stress on issues of self-employment, self-reliance, using the un-used, good leadership, cluster, synergy, convergence.

Some of the issues and priorities which have to be dealt with all holistic seriousness, include the following:

- Image building
- Policies of taxation, training, marketing, monitoring, elections

- Organic, decentralised manufacturing, marketing, production, processing, training, technology, consultancy, coordination centres
- Economy: "eco" - Greek: "oikonomia" = Administrating/ managing a household (good householder)
- Suddenly, in the mid-1990s, the term appeared and caused a real hype in consultancy circles
- Considering human relation factors
- Customer relationship management
- Taskforce(s)
- Participatory rural development
- Youth unemployment
- Infrastructure for rural development
- Knowledge base(s) in villages (+ hidden potentials)
- Developing new products
- Make use of ancient knowledge
- Social entrepreneurship (not harmful to humans + nature)—holistic concept
- Self-fulfilling prophecy
- Unemployment trap
- Importance of good practice: private sector performance *versus* public sector performance
- Women entrepreneurship—separate from general entrepreneurship.

There may be many more areas which will require due attention for marketing the operationalization of development.

We suggest that regular brainstorming be held at all levels to identify and operationalize various problem zones, suggestions, and lessons, for continuous improvement. This will also help in proper monitoring and in avoiding mistakes of the past.

Institution building/Organizational issues

While discussing various issues on operationalization of holistic change, both these terms have a very important role to play. Without getting involved in the dictionary/definition-wise meaning of these words, we assume it as a broad based planning, delivery, monitoring and overall support service provider for holistic change. These include individuals, change agents, monitors, grassroot institutions, media, retired people, trainers and all those associations or federations of stakeholders or role players, along with government, non-government, and semi-government institutions. Since religion, spirituality and community based institutions also play a very important impact-making role, they too, have to be incorporated, whether we like it or not. The purpose of broadening the meaning of these words is to include and give an opportunity to all those who can effectively reduce the cost of operationalization by making it sustainable and all-encompassing.

In matters of institution building and other organizational issues, the Change Agent[1] can be instrumental in facilitating the holistic approach.

Since last two centuries, societies have undergone radical changes with a speed unknown before and still accelerating. The concepts of socialism, capitalism, liberalism, globalization, etc., are much better tested now than ever before. This invariably leds us now to a type of "nature-based", flexible, diversified, seemingly conflicting civilization model. In the process of further search for the ideal conditions for human civilization with peace and development, Gandhiji, Aristotle, Plato, Machiavelli, Hegel, Kant, Einstein, Tolstoy, Vinobaji, Kumarappaji, Kabir, etc., need to be explored anew by a holistic research-action approach. This calls for a network of volunteering, open-minded institutions with the necessary curiosity and urge for exploring the unexplored.

Hence, the following issues or ideas, or questions need to be explored in order to find scientific, analytical, examinable, sustainable answers and directions when it comes to the demand for equity-based, sustainable justice for the world's biodiversity:

1. Have the developmental policies and the institutions created wide chasms between the developed and the so called under-developed?
2. Have the existing institutions and organisations, as broadly understood above, facilitated the realisation of dreams of sustainable human development, or have they collided with exploiters?
3. Can community-based or grassroot institutions identify people's models more effectively and efficiently than the existing institutions?

- "Hypersystem" Village

- Community-based service institutions (grassroot institutions)
- Identifying people's models to disseminate experiences
- Implementable innovative ideas and ideas for productive India
- Defining management in the global vision and local action, challenges of our time
- Strengthening of self-help networks and internal solidarity in agrarian communities: the role of the voluntary sector (NGOs)
- Agricultural investment and the private sector
- Problems of knowledge transfer
- Systems development
- Issues in decentralization
- Transfer as punishment or reward
- "Useless to useful"
- Operationalising best ideas
- Broader context of being, action, non-conformism, issues of differences in naturalness, frauds and conflict, need to be careful and to recognize the un-recognized/network/hobby to profession/back to basics/natural self/determining styles/ work culture/patterns
- Work-Life-Balance
- Resistance towards change
- Identify stakeholders/role players
- Experiences combined with capacities
- Case studies
- and E-based-learning
- Zielsetzung/Zielplanung/Ziele haben damit einen transitorischen Charakter. Sie beschreiben, was eine Organisation, eine Personengruppe oder eine einzelne Person mit den Lern- und Entwicklungsmaßnahmen erreichen will.
- Verhalten: affektiv, kognitiv, psychomotorisch
- Original quotes by Dr. Taori, from his lectures:
  "The poor stays poor, the rich becomes richer."
  "Poverty anywhere is a threat to prosperity anywhere or wherever."

Self-Governance for better attitudes

1. It is the best form of governance, because it is natural, self, total, interdependent, inter-linked, there is a movement, it is understandable because it has a distinct pattern of its own, and it is not greedy nor ambitious.

2. The **I - We - They - Syndrome** is an element of the holistic approach and has high flexibility, autonomy, sensibility, sacrifice.
3. Self-reliance and self-governance are closely related. To face challenges of globalization, it is an imperative that self is allowed to be more and more responsible, accountable, transparent and self-supporting.
4. Self-governance with the right type of trainers facilitates holistic, sustainable development.

Knowledge transfer

The issue of Knowledge Transfer needs to be defined and analysed from at least three different angles:

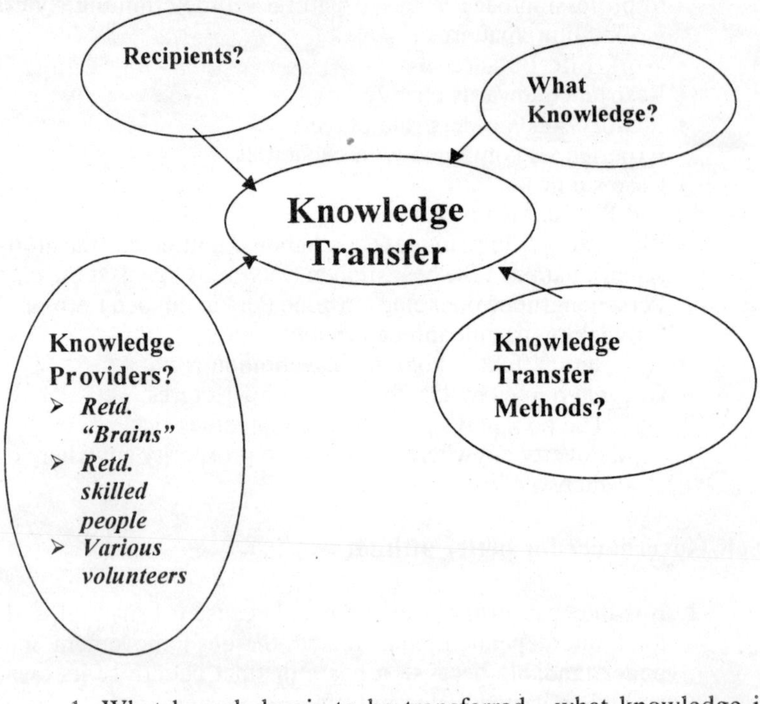

1. What knowledge is to be transferred—what knowledge is required?

2. Who can deliver the required knowledge transfer?
3. Which methods should be applied to achieve efficient knowledge transfer?

Involvement of retired persons is very often a worthwhile endeavour; at the same time, we have to assess that these persons are in tune with the aims and objectives and also, that they were not responsible for the conditions we re fighting against when they were in service.

We also have to stress the various new possibilities of gaining knowledge by new technologies, i.e. the so-called e-learning, which applies in the same way to knowledge transfer.

While examining the knowledge transfer issue, the marketing-led knowledge transfer through business principles or grassroot institutions, or micro-enterprises, or ICT, cannot be neglected. There are many models developed by individual entrepreneurs which are highly effective in knowledge transfer and also, galvanizing the rural investment scenario.

One such model is in practice in Wardha, Maharashtra[2], which is worth being examined for replication. There are many more all over the country, but the authors decided to give only those examples which, in view of their overall performance, come near to our expectations and which they personally could examine. The authors are convinced that there are many more models around us if we start searching for them with open minds.

We have to further encourage and improve existing models and also, schemes, programmes and initiatives which are still in the pipeline. The aim of hope-generating and empowering those still without power, should always be a driving force in our holistic set up.

Summary

While analysing various dimensions of operationalisation, various issues came to the minds of the authors. Depending upon location, problem, issues, expectations and on the whole, requirements of particular time, suitable strategy and action plan has to be developed. Needless to say, there cannot be stereotyped, rigid, inflexible or fixed ideas to be considered; however, depending upon the capacity of the group and the operationaliser, some suggestions can be offered.

For example, in the book *Disaster management through Panchayati Raj*, Dr. Kamal Taori has mentioned the following[3] :

It is high time that we explore better systems of disaster management and Panchayati Raj Institutions as a part of knowledge-based democratic systems of governance. The following plan is suggested for consideration and implementing the suggestions and the finding:

1. A presentation should be made by the undersigned to group of multi-disciplinary participants for widely disseminating and developing a consentized plan of action. This may be organized not only in the training institutions but also selected Ministries/Departments, Inter-State Council, NGOs, Panchayati Raj institutions and even community-based organisations.
2. Many important Ministries and Departments have to reconsider and re-examine their policy, funding, training, R & D, and even monitoring systems. The role of cost-effective, transparent, bankable and viable measures with nearness to people will require changes at various levels. Hence, focused department-wise changes required have to be identified to meet the challenges of disaster and Panchayati Raj empowerment.
3. Selected case studies, hope generating models, policy bottlenecks, lobbying points, convergenistic and bankable project making systems need an effective developmental mindset. Through self-employment and rural investment-oriented bankable schemes with insurance it is possible to attack effectively various areas of disaster provided right and timely policy supports are generated and made available.
4. Missions have to be launched to propel and ignite the dispirited individuals and the institutions. Business-like development through these missions would encourage eco-friendly development and employment-oriented policy development through *asarkari manch*.
5. Role of spiritual institutions, community-based organisations, Panchayati Raj Institutions, training centres, non-resident Indians and people of Indian origin, retired civil and military pensioners, under-utilized and grossly neglected infrastructure and rural resources etc., require a different mindsetting and handling. Hence, documented lessons of the past and compulsions of our time should ignite the under-utilized.
6. The 29 subjects earmarked for Panchayat and self-governance require significant policy and action improvement for overall capacity development of the community and the people to

address various types of disaster. It is here the role of the invisible force, the unrecognizable, the hidden hand, or the luck, also reflected upon.

7. If real India's solid empowerment has to take place, then each Ministry must also have clarity on the mission and the role it is supposed to perform, e.g., Home Ministry must clearly identify short, long and medium-term objectives to be broken into "easily achievable", "impossible to achieve" and "difficult to achieve" targets and sub-targets. Apart from accountability, all those who can help in achieving those targets or likely obstacles need to be documented. It is here the role of NRIs, NGOs, etc., which needs to be documented along with cost and method description of the target achievement.
8. Ultimately villages, towns, communities and rural resources have to be utilized. Hence, a separate Panchayati Raj Ministry along with NGOs and community-based organisations could be converged for better and more effective strategies so that a shift from charity to creativity, capacity and confidence building could be achieved. By laying holistic emphasis on entrepreneurship-led development processes, many of the responsibilities of the government could be easily shared with grassroot institutions of governance. In the same way, many items of expenditure could also be effectively galvanized with the initiative of people and the communities. This will be the best way to unshackle the tremendous energies of the people which are at the moment totally under-utilized. Challenges and imperative compulsions of global vision and local action (GVALA) can easily be achieved if we involve IT and computers with proper motives and the right blend of policies. Needless to say, there are various Investible proposals in each Ministry and Department where entrepreneurs will not seek any fund from government but only supportive policies and hassle-free procedural support. After all, no government should have objections in allowing people to realize their full potential without depending on the State for funds.

We are also convinced that unless we organize the unorganized, market the unmarketed, the concept of holistic disaster management will remain only in theory. "Unless ground level institutions are made to understand their strengths and realize their full potential through their own initiatives, good intentions and local resources, any talk of top-down approach would be equally disastrous."

Regarding the need for adopting market-oriented approach to face the challenges of our time, various suggestions have been given. The compulsions and dimensions of peace along with the role of training and research have also been clearly brought out. By clubbing or effective networking or coordination, many of the issues in operationalisation are solved. This is the natural way of facilitating coordination.

Kamal Taori elaborates on these factors[4] as follows :

Compulsions and Dimensions of Peace

If we accept the challenges of our time and the urgency to look at various strategies and tactics for sustainable peace not only in a few pockets or areas of the world but everywhere, in every nook and corner, then obviously, the massive awakening, the widespread information technology and the free flow of information, also make us to look at various dimensions and compulsions of peace.

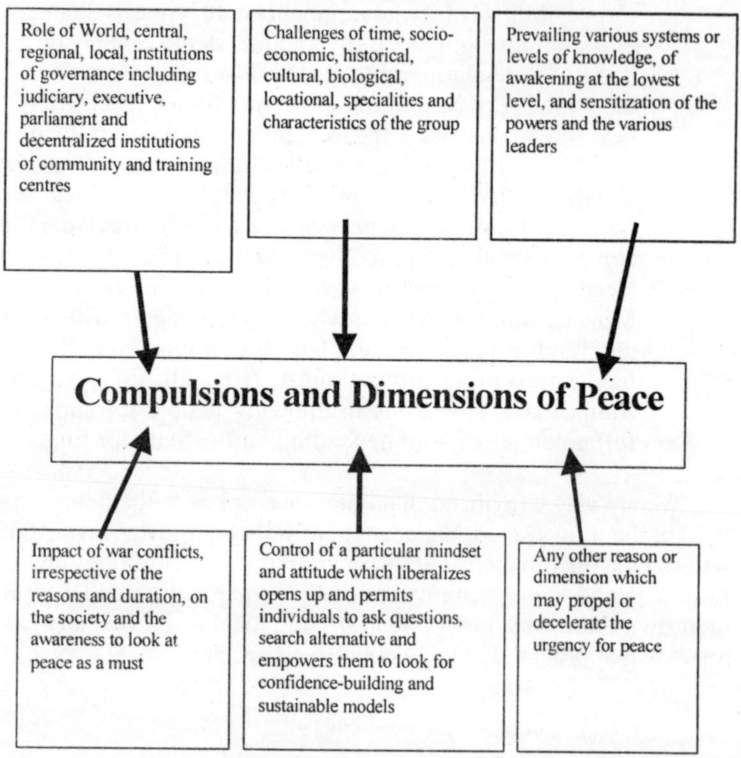

From the above analysis, we will be able to draw some patterns, compulsions, imperatives and also dimensions which will enable us to look into various angles of conflicts, peace and social transformation. This will also facilitate identification of role players and stakeholders, so that long-term and short-term plans of action could be drawn with certain parameters or milestones, checks and balances, and also parameters of success with risk factors.

Role of Training and Research

By compartmentalized treatment of research and training, tremendous harm has been done. The disaster which it has inflicted on the well meaning individuals and also, the society can be corrected only when the aspects of training and research which include codification, planning, learning lessons from others, involving various stakeholders and also carrying out continuous learning and training processes. This also means multi-dimensional approach to analyse, codify, research, training, and continuously take steps to improve the quality of conclusions. Hence, we may look into other dimensions of training and research, going together from the following angles also:

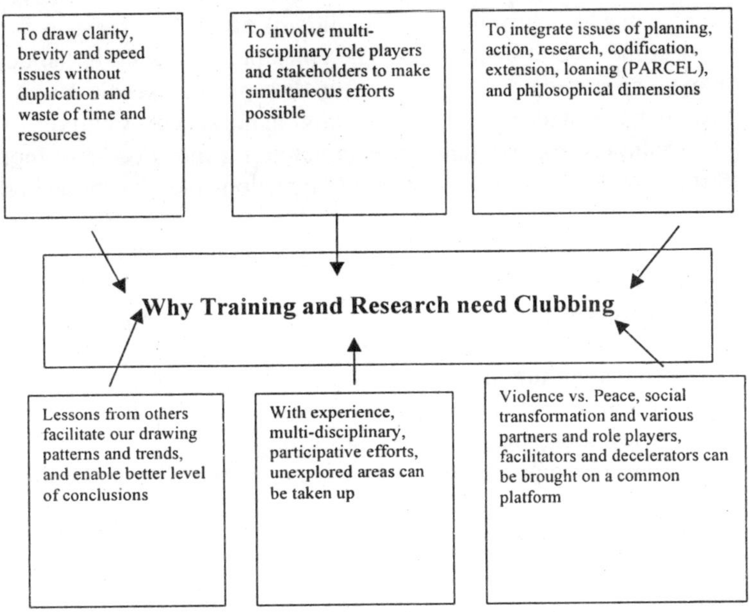

Since compartmentalized approaches by various institutions, professionals, religious and human rights bodies or peace builders, economists, nationalists, financiers, have hardly bothered to come on a common platform and look at the issues holistically, terms like sustainability, strategy, development, quality of life, gross domestic product—vis-à-vis—per capita income, satisfaction and happiness, community, nationhood, state and inter-state relations, etc., need to be explored with different priorities. As challenges of our time keep changing as per region, religion, level of appreciation and knowledge, environmental and locational compulsions, etc., one would find that the issues of clarity, brevity and speed with some other fundamentals of behaviour, satisfaction and the like need to be churned and galvanized.

Working with Individuals and Institutions in the New Context

One feels that it is imperative improving skills and working together, and learning from lessons of the past should be clearly understood in the new context. The fellow and the society have to look into the issues of working with individuals and institutions. The concept of gaining new insight, new data, new theories, new research methods and also, new modes of enquiring for extensively and intensively enriching the conclusions, then the pursuit of peace for the masses may become clearer and clearer. The concept of working in the new context also has many new and unique dimensions. Needless to say, there can be no static parameters for judging the success of this effort. But certainly, some oxygen-like parameters for the success of these efforts can be drawn by asking certain questions like the following:

1. Depending upon the biodiversity, aspirations and the level of knowledge of holistic livelihood, how do the individuals and the society perceive development, peace, training, enterprises and also, policy making instruments?
2. What are the practices in the community and the society to provide best opportunities for every member of the society? May these opportunities be through training, skill upgradations, employment, arts and crafts, business and culture, or even information technology and by utilizing cadres of self-employed mobilizers?

3. What is the communication gap between the organized and unorganized, urbanites and ruralites, those in well paid services and those in self-employed sectors, those working with international bodies and the masses in whose names the linkages are framed, gender issues, children and the aged, and how do religion and spiritual dimensions of living affect the practices of society?
4. How do the professionals perceive their relevancy to their profession and also, to their society?
5. How do scholars, journalists, editors, media and policy-makers, both, at macro- and micro-levels, perceive issues of coordination, linkages, trade, politics, sports, and overall sustainability of higher level of quality of life?
6. In the era of globalization, free trade, borderless states, rising aspirations of the masses, very fast communication and information sharing, how will the information technology and the decentralized systems of governance with policy options be able to contribute to the welfare of the masses on a sustainable basis?

Expected benefits

With the active collaboration and working with seemingly conflicting partners, and with thrust on self-employment and participative investment, the issues of peace, social transformation and removal of conflicts avoidance will definitely get clarity.

It is only after clarification that the issues of dissemination, training and further improvement for better systems development and management is possible. The role of NGOs as complementary civic institutions have hardly been utilized in the Third World Countries. The NGOs can transform the dormant lowest level political institutions into vibrant agencies of social and economic empowerment of the people. Globalization and localisation issues can very well be treated with the active partnership of the NGOs. It is here that networking, global vision and local action could facilitate a win-win situation for all, resulting in peace, sustainability and development. It is also a fact that NGOs and other training institutions have been working in isolation. It is high time, as resources become scarce and the demand ever-increasing, that these opportunities are utilized to provide cost-effective self-employment-oriented extension and replication systems. It is here that the organisations of communities, the society of professionals and the bureaucracy have to learn to produce, churn and disseminate knowledge and skills with speed and effectiveness. Needless to say, seminars, workshops, brainstorming sessions, case studies, local area planning and resources mapping, together with conflict resolution and peace stabilization efforts could be very useful.

Once these efforts are set on the right path and are widely accepted, then certain additional efforts are required to make these efforts widely known through edited volumes, news media, conferences, websites, policy workshops and also, sensitization of policy-makers and leaders at various levels.

How the Training Research Initiatives contribute to Newness or Plan of Action and Churning Processes :

1. As mentioned earlier, various isolated, dispersed initiatives have been taken to a compartmentalized look into issues of social transformation, peace and conflict. Hence, by bridging of different bodies of knowledge and theory produced by researchers and by involving various NGOs and role players.
2. We have to encourage performance by local initiatives, recognition and incentives with rewards.
3. Learning to working together on area basis with transparency, viability and win-win situation.
4. Panchayat, community, NGO, IT and marketing-led compulsions have to be involved.
5. Role of vegetarianism, health, food, broadening of mindset and attitude development have to be converged.
6. Issues of self-employment, rural investment and business-like principles of good governance, accountability and value for money need cost-effective treatment.
7. There is overstaffing, very poor work culture, lack of transparency in most of the institutions, both, in government and outside government. Even the private sector has been a miserable failure. Hence, a climate or an environment or an overall thrust has to be galvanized for better performance-oriented systems.

8. The greatest problem is that of leadership at every level, whether it is permanent or temporary, rural or urban, economic or social, developmental or regulatory, HRD or any other field.
9. The utter frustration, cynicism, hopelessness, purposelessness and lack of direction prevalent all around need to be converted into an opportunity by accepting the challenge. Small initiatives should lead to policy changes and better public administration and governance.
10. Stereotyped workshops, conferences, brainstorming sessions, must shift to a result-oriented output, based on previous codified levels of knowledge. The entire scheme of things seems to be budget-utilization-oriented. This has to undergo radical change through **"I - WE - THEY"**- initiatives.
11. The need to encourage example setting processes by reducing the gap between the precept and the practice.
12. Innovations in thinking and implementation need to be made a part of annual reports of all departments. This should also include the areas of weakness and how societies, NGOs, IT-facilities, communities and entrepreneurs could come forward to remove bottlenecks.

Volunteering and Challenges

When we look at various aspects of governance, research, funding, man-management and overall development of various disciplines, we find an increasing role for volunteering as a mission. Some religions already compel their members to become volunteers and also share resources as part of their system build-up. The philanthropists, spiritually and volunteering, have been enmeshed and are inseparable. Governments all over the world are also propelling the causes of volunteering.

The question is to examine the issues of **Niyat** (motivator), **Niti** (policy), and **Niyati** (destiny). By neglecting the study of these three issues, volunteering has developed as a business or as a grant-using mechanism. Without any system of follow-up monitoring, cost effective analyses and on the whole systems of cross-check volunteering has also earned the same bad name. it is high time that the following issues are holistically examined to come to a proper role-placing for volunteering.

In this evaluation process, Gandhiji has a lot to offer by way of prescriptions and modalities so that a holistic analysis is possible. It is here, the lessons of the past and the miserable collapse of many of the volunteering programmes, even started by Gandhiji, need to be critically examined. Many institutions which Gandhiji, Vinobaji and many more well-meaning people started, have ultimately faced the same fate due to certain missing elements which would give sustainable meaning to volunteering. Aspects like growth, humanity, attention to neglected, communication with unorganized, comparative cost analysis, marketing-driven development policies, cost-effective systems of servicing and governance, allowing entrepreneurial systems for the masses and self-employment, paying attention to local resources and knowledge with skills, etc., have to be reviewed.

Volunteering has a lot of emerging investment opportunities with reference to neglected areas, groups, programmes, people. The challenges of our time exhort us to look at the following challenges posed before the volunteers:

(a) How can government and its institutions benefit from the experiences, expertise and visions of the volunteering sector?
(b) Can governments and their departments bring out areas of concern and exhort reasonable participation with policies and effects contribution from the volunteering sector?
(c) Wherever governments have failed miserably, can they have the courage to accept frankly and invite grassroot institutions, communities and people to converge with IT and volunteers?
(d) Resources with the State should be basically for the people. The vested interests and the well entrenched centres of exploitation have to be countered by raising sensitised policy-making level of government, non-government and communities. How do we go about it?
(e) Emerging opportunities of investment in neglected sectors can be effective only if transparency, right to information, bankability, marketing, etc., are fully converged. This means again new emerging vistas and visions for volunteering.

Strategy for Improvement

Many feel that we are in a war-like situation. As war needs strategy and is focused on pooling of resources, the same way peace also requires a "war strategy". Volunteering based upon experiences of Gandhiji will also need a war-like strategy. This means, the whole training, funding, grooming, financing, motivating, planning, and even role clarification will have to undergo radical change.

Instead of changing the rulers, parties, or the laws, the need will be analyse the basic issues of civilization. Those used to exploitative systems of governance have to be mentally and attitudinally motivated to examine their situation from a different angle.

If we look at the present-day condition of this world as a whole, the term **"slaughterhouse"** is the only one which can be realistically used to describe it. In a true Gandhian spirit, we cannot leave it like that. Many might say that till now, all peace initiatives, peace movements, all efforts to bring people closer to each other, thus bringing about global understanding and an end to atrocities, have miserably failed. The authors are well aware of that. But, at the same time, we all would contribute to the downfall of all civilization if we do not stand up and fight with all the weapons we can muster. The enemies of mankind are those who perpetuate exploitation, those who stand in the way of controlling overpopulation, those who still produce and sell arms and ammunition and those who force human beings to use them. The enemies of mankind are those who for their personal gains suppress the rights of others, those who are irreparably destroying nature, deliberately out of greed or because they are not able to grasp the consequences of their actions. The enemies of mankind are corrupt politicians and bureaucrats everywhere, mis-user of otherwise useful infrastructure, governments which are prepared to compromise on almost everything, provided they stay in power or else, foreign money continues to flow.

But, at the same time, our "enemies of mankind" are our own brothers and sisters. How to deal with them? How to convince them that they destroy their own very roots? We are not utopist enough to think that this can be an easy task. We are convinced that we will not live to see peace on earth and welfare for all. But, we are determined to join the fight with those who are likeminded to dedicate themselves to fighting non-violently but efficiently.

The role of holistic examination in the challenging time will require a transformation on practical fields. Wherever success has been acclaimed, it has to be examined again holistically. Parameters of testing have to stand the test of time, cost-effectiveness, win-win for all and many more vital issues. The authors suggest the following plan of action which should be considered for holistic planning of action and research.

A Plan of Action for Facing the Challenges

1. Lots of good models are available all over the country. Efforts should be made to codify and examine them holistically. A national mission to search for good initiatives is urgently required.
2. Panchayati Raj Institutions, community, NGOs, have important roles to play in facing the challenges of our time. Senior Gandhians must encourage youth and emerging leaders from all walks of life to experiment and venture into unchartered areas.
3. Issues of policies, training attitude, mindset, marketing, technology extension and even convergence, require multi-disciplinary action research. It is high time that regional transparent models are replicated.
4. A lot of research is being done but has hardly any relevancy. Hence, issues of regional and local priorities must find relevancy in all these researches.
5. The system of governance seems to have become irrelevant. Issues of cost effectiveness, confidence building of the people, transparency, etc., need to be attended to with new approaches. Gandhian institutions, spread all over the country, could encourage new leadership and also develop the mindset for good governance.
6. Small rewards, returns, and incentives have to be propagated so that awareness increases from bottom.
7. Under-utilized infrastructure with all the institutions needs to be converged and properly utilized for self-employment and rural investment missions.
8. The issues of self-reliance, self-confidence, reflection and, on the whole, the issue of mindsetting, require continuous search and research. Senior Gandhians must reflect upon good and bad points of post-independence and offer viable, Implementable suggestions.
9. Planning from bottom has remained neglected. The training institutions, Panchayati Raj Institutions, NGOs and

self-employed rural mobilizers must pool their resources. A National Mission on volunteering and action must be integrated with various non-performing institutions. Volunteering in all walks of life must be systematized. Local resources, skills and expertise have to be converged for grass-root confidence building.

10. Neglected programmes of market and welfare of all have to be made into free programmes.
11. From economic development to holistic development will require a lot of initiative and effort. Whether it is training, research, funding, election or any other field of human activity, the cohesive forces must be unleashed. From authoritative democratic leadership, a lot of effort will be required.
12. Lessons of history need to be properly codified. Issues of holistic training, research and development as a part of Hind Swaraj must be regularly examined.
13. Youth holds the key to the tomorrow. They must be encouraged, guided and properly advised so that the time is activated. The brand name GHANDHI, the qualities of patience, perseverance, consistency and inspiration have to be made into a part of life. The gap between precept and practice needs to be bridged. It is only through proper analyses and action that better performers can emerge. He connection between good means and good ends has to be again re-established.
14. A continuous reflection series, both, individually and collectively, is the urgency of our time. Panchayati Raj Institutions and rural activisation would all be successful only if serious commitment to performance is ensured.

Summing up

One would like to say that the challenges of our time compel us to bring on a common platform both, young and old. It is high time that the lessons of the past are churned to draw better guiding principles and oxygen points for tomorrow's action.

To face the challenges of our time, we have to organize properly and naturally. Nature has to guide our planning and action. Limitations of our planet have to always be kept in mind. The Gandhian agenda for the twenty-first century also, exhorts us to think of the real India, i.e. rural India. It is a difficult task, but it has to be accomplished.

In another book authored by Dr. Kamal Taori: "People's Participation in Sustainable Human Development (A Unified Search)", he has raised some questions which need to be analysed and deeply probed. These include

1. How the programmes run by UN system, World Bank, and people themselves benefited larger target groups?
2. How do the lessons meet time test for success?
3. Are they replicable? How, when, where, why?
4. Are they sustainable? How and why?
5. Are they cost effective? How?
6. Are they eco-friendly? How?
7. Do they help shift people from charity to creativity, capacity and confidence-building process?
8. Do they help in self-development?
9. Do they help in repaying capacity building of the institution?
10. Do they help in developing brotherhood, feeling of unity and broaden vision in the masses for overall happiness?

In this context, we should always keep in mind that :

> ***"Happiness is not something ready made. It comes from your own actions."***
>
> (Dalai Lama)

It is high time that all the policies, systems, procedures and practices are researched. The globalisation imperative and compulsion of local strengthening compel us to look at the past experiences with holistic mindset. The parameters itself may have to be re-examined because some of the following challenges of our time do not offer easy solutions :

1. Massive aspirations to do something. It is here each individual feels committed to do something of his own.
2. Easy availability of focussed communication through Radio TV, Fax, Computer with comparatively much better infrastructure.

3. Cost structure is an important force both for services, recruitment and practical weight.
4. 30 per cent women are essential for Panchayati Raj bodies.
5. All round resource scarcity.
6. Over-dependence of State.
7. Deteriorating working standards.
8. Lack of transparency and replicability.
9. World movement towards eco-friendliness (environment protection).
10. Re-emergence and re-engineering of issues relating to development.
11. Ills of organised industries becoming clear.
12. Need to develop replicable models.
13 Failure of earlier acclaimed successful models.
14. Realising need to restructure marketing.
15. Growing international interest in Gandhi's Philosophy and concern of Globalisation and Self-Reliance.
16. Ongoing restructuring of financial, legal and administrative institutions.
17. Dwindling of industrial resources.
18. Ever increasing population.
19. Climate change.

While local, national and international bodies and institutions have been trying find operationalizable strategies and tactics for effectively solving the challenges of our time, one cannot rule out the necessity for looking into the following:

1. Re-defining multi-dimensionally various definitions.
2. De-mystifying various established concepts and value systems.
3. Keeping in mind the cross-cultural differences developing models to suit vision of tomorrow.
4. Realizing more and more on rationalistic, scientific analysis, analytical approach rather than borrowed implanted concepts.
5. Decentralised Government and involvement of all with Panchayati Raj systems as institutional local governance.

In the effort to integrate "Parliamentarians Forum" with local bodies and other ongoing programmes as a part of New Economic

Policy, various issues have been taken up by Dr. Kamal Taori. The challenges are so deep-rooted that the blueprint of any operationalization of change must include general and also specific issues. The biggest difficult areas are of coordination, cooperation, and co-existence in a diverse world. The transparency and availability compulsions make permanent civil servants active partners with politicians in exploitation. Hence, UN systems and various agencies have to consider that even in their own systems, there are various problems of co-ordination. The funding systems have miserably failed in improving the lot of the masses. The traditional systems are hand-in-glove with established funders to grab the cream. Thus, the people must be involved with enthusiasm and optimism by integrating the policies. The common problems which need attention include the following:

1. High cost—low impact.
2. Lack of involvement of actual beneficiaries by contributing labour resources—long-term risks.
3. Initiative of local people neglected.
4. Lack of Marketing Culture with self-employment opportunities.
5. Basic policy weaknesses for convergence and use of unused.
6. Missing links for replicability, transparency and availability.

Involving local organizations, institutions, bodies, governments, media, bankers, etc., for effective operationalization of grassroot development plans:

1. Any plan of Action has to be area-based, say, a village or a community.
2. The felt need of the people, specially from demand angle needs proper appreciation. Hence, whatever is going out from the village must be stored, value added and marketed at the best price. On the other hand, whatever comes from outside, should be locally developed wherever possible.
3. There is need to involve all local leaders and initiatives in the action projections. Their co-operation and co-ordination needs codification with appreciation.

4. SWOT analyses and HIPPOO, KIPPOO, TIPPOO, FIPPOO, GIPPOO, DIPPOO[5] of the area would make the job much easier for analyses on action, investment, employment, and environment protection.
5. Training has to be on practical basis.
6. Monitoring systems should be based on regular interaction with multi-disciplinary teams including banks.
7. Emerging areas or viable investment, self-employment and policy packages need sharing.
8. In the world of greed-led growth, there is the need to plan fruit-eating versus root-eating. Values like honesty, transparency, and reward for hard work should be encouraged. In the liberalized economy, thirst on localization and self-reliance has to be properly appreciated.
9. The quality level of leadership at grassroot needs to be fully harnessed by mindsetting, attitudes, case studies and showing models in the same conditions. Local leadership institutions with emphasis on turnkey consultancy, follow-up of results including monitoring, suitable marketing and micro-funding provisions can go a long way to bring out the best of local development plans.
10. Those who have gone away from rural areas need to be encouraged to either come back or co-operate with the ruralites.

Above, these are only a few selected suggestions which can galvanize rural areas. Many institutional, structural, policy and mindset-related radical changes have to be ushered in to solve various problems and challenges of our time. There are no shortcuts to quality programmes. Hence, a continuous search has to go on.

Building good Institutions for Operationalising Effective Change

In the era of intense competition, it is imperative that building good institutions receives due attention. The ever changing needs of market, governance, aspirations of the people require institutions capable of meeting the challenges just in time. The angles of productivity, cost reduction, win-win for all, socio-economic aspects of development.

Needless to say that poorly performing institutions and organisations leave disastrous systems and impacts on civil society. To face the challenges of our time, stereotyped mindset, training modules, compartmentalized policies, are bound to play havoc. Thus, for Operationalising effective, sustainable, transparent and replicable change, we have to consider elements essential for building good institutions.

For our purposes, institutions and organisations facilitate the enhancement and optimization of naturally endowed capacities bestowed so lavishly by nature. Whether it is individual or community, or society, or region, emphasis has to be on developing and enabling environment protection. This means the role of institutions has to encompass the divergent needs of so called development on the one side, and meeting the challenges of the future on the other.

Building good institutions therefore has to look into the following issues:

1. What are the holistic change issues to be attended?
2. What have been the lessons of the past?
3. Who are the people to benefit and what is their contribution?
4. Who are the managers, promoters, organizers?
5. How would the issues of clarity, brevity and speed be shared?
6. What would be the training, monitoring, coordinating needs?
7. What would be the infrastructural requirements of marketing and networking?
8. What special features would be required for the unorganized, decentralized and dispersed socio-economic sectors?
9. While defining and grading good institutions, how parameters like location, capacity utilization, participation of neglected groups, internal resource generation, bank finance, vision, training, marketing, accountability, documentation, women's involvement, environment protection, etc., can be utilized?
10. Unfortunately, many sustainable changes can never come through local interventions. Hence, suggestions from top like Planning Commission, PMO, Finance Ministry, etc., would definitely usher in compulsion for local improvisation. Can these instil dynamism and propel the dormants to become self-activated by coming out of their shell of complacency?
11. Can improvements come in isolation? Hence, can movements,

missions, lobbying, networking, media, social audits and effective turnkey consultancies become imperative?

12. Can the role of volunteering and going beyond self-interests be re-defined and made influential by brainstorming, tours, workshops, sharing of experiences, networking, improved target-setting with effective HRD methods?
13. Can continuous learning and documenting be part of the system or atmosphere?
14. How should the Series of Performer's Presentation or Marketing the Unmarketed, or Organizing the Unorganized be a part of the system development?
15. How can mid-term corrections and timely interventions save institutions from collapsing? Since enough characteristics, indications, symptoms, tests, if properly noticed and deciphered, definitely corrective steps can be initiated in time.
16. Can Self Employed Change Agents (SECA)—type of social activist cadre be developed to facilitate the building up of institutions by providing holistic consultancy services like turnkey consultancy, marketing concepts, networking support, IT knowledge transfer, etc.?

REFERENCES

1. see "Village Change Agent".
2. see Appendix: Series of Performers Presentations of Hope Models, by one of the authors, Dr. Taori.
3. Dr. Kamal Taori, *Disaster Management Through Panchayati Raj,* pp 15-17.
4. *Ibid.,* pp 138-47.
5. see Glossary.

Chapter-16

EPILOGUE

In this book, both the authors have tried to express their concerns, their experiences and the options from an operationalizable angle. We were strongly motivated and challenged by many philosophers through all ages and from East and West. The term "philosophy" and "philosopher" is precisely defined as "love for knowledge" or else, "one who loves knowledge". Transported into our modern language, we can say that philosophy applies to those who question and are in search for or provide answers. As we understand it from our holistic approach, philosophy comprises thinking and questioning in abstractions, realities and in action.

We are also convinced that the problems of development are so intermingled with all sciences that any compartmental approach, as against our holistic concept, is bound to lead to failure and further disaster. Unfortunately, research and development are mainly conducted under a totally compartmentalized approach.[1]

Professionals and experts have miserably failed in solving the problems of society permanently. Hence, with the aim of **marketing the un-marketed**, the people have to be brought forward.

On this background, we would like to appeal to the concerned readers to think and ponder over the following questions:

1. Have we involved our elected representatives at all levels as democratically responsible leaders? Have we followed the basic requirements of a vibrant democracy? Many feel that in reality it is a facade going on in the name of vibrant and transparent democracy. Are we as a vibrant nation really doing and achieving the best from our potentials? Are we an over-centralised, over-governed, over-bureaucratised type of a non-performing society?
2. Have we learned from the performers or from those self-employed entrepreneurs who are not dependent on grants? Can we draw lessons from the success case studies given in the annexure?

3. Have we codified investments of the past and made full use? Actually, most of the construction works has been funded, contracted, supervised, and finally paid for by Central or State government and local people or their institutions had hardly anything to do with it. No wonder, a lot of infrastructure in all departments is laying waste. Can local people takeover and use these?
4. As in point 3, in addition to the waste in the infrastructural side, more often than not the constructions themselves were not apt to serve the needs of the local people. Can anything be done here to make good use of it?
5. **"Nutrimentum spiritus"** is written on the prestigious building of the Humboldt University in Berlin, Germany, named after the famous Philosopher and educational reformer. Where is the **food for thought** or the **nutrition** for our **spirit** today? Wherever you look, hope models are missing in our thinking and writing. The darkness areas need to be lightened up. The society, the individuals, each one of us has to do brain-storming, constant evaluation of one's potentials and actual realisation. For accomplishing this process we need facilitators at all levels of society. Is our society really promoting these types of institutions of performance? If yes: how and where, and if no: then, why not? Whom do we blame for these unexcusable mistakes?
6. Are we really proud of outstanding achievements and have they really benefited the masses? There are many who are outstandingly performing in the same system. Are we, if at all we can be called a caring society, then really bothered about doing something to improve the systems?
7. Are the policies really empowering people to act in their own interests? The authors went through various books dealing with pre-Islamic, British periods, Post-British periods and recent literature on the happenings around India and the world. The bibliography mentions some books which will benefit any serious reader and student of contemporary time. How do we draw lessons from all these known, well researched and documented books for the future? It is appalling to read and know the findings and observe how the same mistakes are being constantly repeated. Mr. Romesh Dutt, a well-known ICS and outstanding historian, has brought out the

nature of all round exploitation of India by the Britishers both, during East India Company days and during the Colonial Government. The prescription by the author is most interesting. In his book written some time in 1901, "THE ECONOMIC HISTORY OF INDIA",[2] he has advocated the involvement of some representatives as the answer or, in the longer run, self rule as the answer. Now, after so many decades of total independence and so-called vibrant democracy and elections, do we realise what sort of civil, egalitarian, enlightened, public-spirited, dedicated to welfare of the masses, systems of governance we are having? Should we be ashamed or proud?

8. Have we made people beggars and destitute by creating a mindset of grants and subsidies? Has the still prevalent middle class mindset with its centuries of starvation in all aspects of life, with the pseudo-moralistic imposed values in day-to-day behaviour, with its suppression of natural needs and hopes, made us a greedy, careless, egoist, overconfident, loot-eating, distrustful society? Why do we give up our identity by sacrificing our dignity, our natural cultural patterns to the gods of wealth, mainly from the West? Whether we like it or not, we are a multi-peopled, multi-cultural, multi-religious, multi-language, etc., society, but the chances of a harmony is becoming more and more disbalanced. The rigidity of fundamentalism from all sides, with its disrespect to others, its insensitivity, its ruthless cruelties and violence, will tear the society apart in civil wars all over the country. The only answer to efficiently stand up against this development is the revival of Gandhian thoughts, modernize and transferring them into the minds of the people and shaping and activating them holistically. How can we reach the masses?
9. The process of sustainable consensus-building resulting in lasting harmonious relationship is one of the most difficult tasks. Even two people with adequate sympathy, adequate level of knowledge and similar interests, may often find it difficult to harmonize. India with its ancient civilization and richness of culture, arts and crafts, and wisdom, could not tolerate Buddhism, so that it became almost extinct from the soil of India. It was only late Dr. Ambedkar who revived Buddhism in India. We shudder to think: what would have

> happened to India if he had embraced Islam of Christianity? History is proof of the fact that both the religions have aggressively and violently marketed themselves. With a holistic approach to diversity, is it not necessary that the Indian systems should be developed on scientific, rational, analytical, philosophical and also, practical levels, instead of only power-greedy, stereotyped systems in almost all strata of society? Can a promising beginning be made in time? Do we not feel that the areas of duplicity, hypocrisy, poor imagination, accessibility, secrecy, sexual taboos, require a holistic re-thinking at all levels if disaster is to be avoided?

The questions above are only a few from so many which we put at random to enable interested readers to get deeper intc the context of development with holistic approach. In the following, we elaborate on some more issues which will be taken up in the forthcoming series of books by the authors. For example:

Law and Order

Up till now, everybody has tried to tackle this problem in isolation, but law and order problems have to be solved **holistically**. Unless we involve all stakeholders and decentralize the decision-making, all will fail.

The structures of governance have become top-heavy. Apart from enhancing the efficiency, we have to make them cost-effective in a way which will have repercussions in the behavioural field. It is a fact that those working at the front are at the bottom of the salary ladder whereas those who do not have to put much effort in their work are the well-paid ones. This is perceived as in-just and thus highly demotivating.

Unconventional models of restructuring the hierarchies, the pay-structure and other fields of concern after merit and the actual demands of work and the workload have to be developed and introduced. As the law and order situation is a highly personnel-oriented issue, we are facing the problem of time running out as all changes in personnel matters require lots of time till results are improved.

The greatest area of concern is not only the inordinate delay in comprehending the seriousness of the indifference of those in power, but also of the lack of corrective desire. The permanent bureaucracy which was to provide this bridge has proved to be highly selfish and used to perks of the permanent power and privileges. It all comes back to the vicious circle of those wielding power and those who do not: those, once having grappled power use it to consolidate, at the same time preventing everybody else to intervene. Those who cannot wield power submit to the seemingly inevitable. This way, everything repeats itself, and power structures remain the same as they were — **no chance for breaking this vicious circle**. This means that the law-and-order-authorities, as part of the system, cannot have any interest for themselves to bring about a change which, in the first place, might be of disadvantage to them.

In a backward society like in India this makes problems worse and worse.

Hence, we request all concerned to consider the following:

1. Do we have **performers** around us in any walk of life. If so, can we use, study write about them so that good models are taken up for studies and hope multiplying?
2. The challenges of our time have to be constantly evalued and taken up for action. There are no shortcuts. The lessons of history of the world in general and India in particular can also teach us a lot for action. There are well documented experiments even by great performers like Gandhiji. Can we negate the importance of lessons of peace, non-violence, truth, tolerance, etc. ?
3. How do we fight the cause of nature and holistic developments without getting exterminated?
4. Can the violent nature of war by the so-called most powerful world nations be forgotten so easily?
5. How can the knowledge of Buddha, Mahavira and Christ in the original sense be neglected if humanity is not to be extinct?
6. Some of the other most serious challenges before the world include

    - Over population
    - Corruption, insensitivity of those in power, persistent failure of so called developmental programmes, gaps between precept and practice
    - Fundamentalism of all types
    - Inordinate delay in implementing the known

- Lack of awareness of good works done or being done, Persistent neglect of merit of all kinds
- Too much compartmentalisation and avoidable over-cost of governance
- Over exploitation of nature, speedy, irreparable loss of bio-diversity
- Self-righteousness of the wealthy, the spiritual, religious, etc.
- Lack of vision: be it short-term or long-term, lack of flexibility in thinking and planning.

India, after our holistic analysis of potentials and possibilities, is in a comparative advantageous position where it could offer and show to the world a different, sustainable, vibrant and win-win model if it does not depend upon the planners of our destiny. This requires a new, different, questioning mind with right attitudes. We would like to have full confidence that the old or new generation would not repeat or allow others to repeat the mistakes which the world is committing with impunity. What is essentially required is the massive mass awakening in the younger generation at all levels.

What happened to the courage and commitment of the Indian people which has been so very much there during freedom struggle? Where has this attitude vanished? Why do we have a society of timids, sycophants, hypocrites, apes…

The basic mistakes for the utterly disastrous development of Indian society have been made in the first 10 to 20 years after independence, when Gandhiji's vision of an egalitarian, decentralised, multi-faceted society was literally buried and forgotten. Gandhiji's vision was thrown unto the garbage-heap of history by the politicians. The same people who took advantage by calling themselves "Gandhians", but were prepared to compromise for the sake of short-term gains. The gods of industrialization, urbanisation, Westernisation, and much more, were added to the big pantheon of Hindu gods and goddesses and properly revered. All this on the cost of the masses who felt all their expectations unfulfilled and became more and more dis-illusioned and finally lost all hope. The change from white sahibs to brown sahibs meant no change at all for them; in the meantime, the lot of the rural poor is even worse than 40 or 50 years back.

What happened to all the courageous, committed freedom fighters after they came into positions of power and money? Why did most of them yield to the temptations of power and money? Why did they stop fighting for a just and egalitarian society? One of the very few former freedom fighters we had the opportunity to talk openly about these questions told the authors frankly: "We had spent hard times. We thought it just to be rewarded. We rewarded ourselves and forgot our cause."

REFERENCES

1. As in almost all schools and academic institutions, governmental structures, and other set ups.
2. 1st Indian edition in 1960.

Appendix-I

1. **Case Study** of an NGO: **XYZ**. The methods of analysis and also, the issues of concern can be applied to all NGOs and to similar organisations or institutions. In the already described **flexible system of modules** (like in leadership training, SECA training, etc.), here, the basic ten criteria or modules can be removed, exchanged with other criteria, or other criteria can be added according to the special type or requirement of the institution. At the same time, these criteria/modules with their methods of acquiring data and evaluating them (not shown below) can be used for proper grading or self-grading of an institution.

NGO XYZ (Evaluation, analyses and summary)

The authors evaluated and analyzed a number of existing NGOs and pooled together their findings in short interpretations. Not astonishingly, the overall problems and areas of concern are widely identical, also the fact that almost all of them are suffering under the same disease of stunning passivity.

I. ***Style of functioning***

We observed certain patterns in the style of functioning which are clearly adverse to build-up sustainable development of the institutions. The main obstacles are shown in the following:

1. lack of transparency in almost all spheres, especially in decision-making and finances.
2. pseudo-democratic:

   - community meetings are conducted, but the real issues are not discussed
   - decisions are hardly discussed, but facts might be communicated after
   - personnel decisions are not democratically taken
   - often: relatives and/or family members of founders or

other important persons are given positions for which the are not qualified.

3. decision-making is too slow.
4. lack of reliability (time-wise and quality-wise).
5. lack of organisationally efficient work plan, so that personnel is hired without having work to do, whereas on other places, workforce is not available.
6. lack of flexibility in fully using the existing infrastructure, including the personnel potentials.

II. ***Cost consciousness***

In view of the overall lack of financial resources, the authors were stunned by their observations of clear wastage of money. The main observations are shown below:

1. money squandering through lack of control mechanisms:

    - calculations are often done out of the blue without clear cost estimates
    - external workers are hired without clear cost agreements
    - no system of obligatory comparative cost estimates is observed
    - maintenance of buildings, machines, and other maintenance-sensitive equipment is neglected
    - furnishings, fittings and materials are not properly kept so that they are rotting away.

2. money squandering through keeping people in positions for which they are not qualified.
3. no suitable infrastructure nor halfway proper plan is designed for creating backup funds systematically in cases of recurring works or cases of "emergencies", like urgent renovation work, unforeseen expenses, etc.

III. ***Resources***

In all institutions, we found material and immaterial resources in abundance, but they were hardly used fully, not to mention those which are not even recognized nor tapped at all. It seems that the donors who always rushed to help and supported extension of projects or new ones (if the old ones failed), are mainly responsible for this attitude. There seems to be no pressure of identifying and using all resources available. In the following, we show the main findings:

1. due to the above-mentioned lack of cost consciousness, and due to the absence of an infrastructure for checking resources and efficiency, many valuable resources are not efficiently used, like

    - regularly checking different electricity tariffs for saving possibilities
    - hospitals without qualified personnel where equipment is rotting away
    - roads without traffic
    - schools without teachers
    - industrial sheds and other buildings with no industries
    - skills of personnel which are not used, etc.

2. financial resources are sometimes used for purposes other than they are meant for; this creates an impression of incredibility by the donors which could prompt them to give up donating altogether.
3. products are manufactured without marketability or, marketable products are not marketed due to lack of proper efforts, thus scarce resources are frittering away.

IV. ***Attitudes***

In every community or institution, the overall attitude towards work efficiency is dependent on the credibility and the ability to motivate, in short: on the quality of leadership. In our research, we observed a change of attitude which had been evolved during the last decades, as all changes in attitudes normally need a certain time span. In our special cases, it is very clear that with the ageing of the founder-fathers and subsequently their diminishing influence and function as motivators and role models, the overall attitude within the institutions went towards indifference, even hostility. These are extremely alarming facts.

The following shows the main findings:

1. loss or shifting away of the original ideas of the mission and the philosophy of the institution, like, for example, in the educational field, a former lively Gandhian spirit, or, in the field of health, the shift towards commercializing the service instead of serving the poor, etc.
2. widespread sloppiness ("Just-so"-syndrome): time-wise and quality-wise, due to absence of work evaluation and also, absence of proper guidance in work ethics.
3. personnel is not given sufficient qualification so that many cannot deliver proper work even when they have the determination to do so; seminars and workshops for improving skills and work ethics are not conducted.
4. due to the overall feeling that money has always come from all sorts of sources, the consciousness of the value of working for money is almost nil.

V. *Personnel*

In the personnel field, the authors had the most negative impressions. Most of the staff are going about their work in a nonchalant way, not really committed, with a work discipline which would not be allowed in any private company. Be it in matters of punctuality or reliability, be it in matters of understanding the cause of the institution, most of the staff is deplorably negligent.

The following shows our main findings:

1. Unfortunately, most of the founder-fathers forgot to build-up a solid second-line leadership in time. This led to a deplorable state of second-rate might-be successors with limited skills, almost no charismatic personalities and thus, very little natural authority within the institution. Besides, the fact of in-fights for succession is raging in some institutions which takes away much needed energies for actual work.
2. In almost all institutions, we observed a comparatively high personnel fluctuation, especially by younger, highly skilled staff. Our inquiries with those who left resulted mainly in: lack of career perspectives, responsible positions are blocked by retired persons, no appreciation or motivation, lack of transparency, injustice in salary structure, no transparency in decision-making, no orientation into future developments,

insecurity in view of the dependency of the institution from grants and donations.

3. In spite of the existence of many skilled personnel and among them, quite a lot of younger staff, we found no concept for systematically developing their abilities, for identifying their potentials and strengths, for training them in various fields needed in the institution. What we found instead was the constant complaint of lack of certain skills and abilities and the need for finding retired persons to fill the gaps, considering the costs.
4. We could hardly find a system for fixing salaries, except perhaps in educational institutions with the teachers, but even there, it has been difficult to recognize. Salaries are not transparent and are very often considered as unjust. The fact that often non-performers keep their positions for years and years together, even execute power over better skilled staff, is considered as rewarding non-performance and punishing good work. Thus, the best leave, the others stay.

VI. *Administration*

Instead of good management, we found in most of the institutions an overwhelming set up of administrative stumbling blocks, a maze of rules and regulations of no recognizable sense, in short: a bureaucratic hydrocephalus which can be found in every government establishment, too.

In the following, we show the main findings:

1. over-bureaucratization.
2. lack of transparency in accountancy and other matters.
3. stickling to petty rules and regulations, but sloppiness on cost-relevant issues.
4. by prolonging procedures, putting up formal stumbling blocks and punishing trespassers, self-initiative and creativity are mercilessly killed.

VII. *Organisation patterns*

As mentioned in the preceding para, over-bureaucratization can cause many obstacles and dangers. We got the impression that, as in many organisations, the administration, which actually should serve as a supporting agent in the background, crept step by step into the most powerful position where nothing could move any more without its consent. And, we all know, in the clutches of administration nothing moves any more.

The following shows our main findings:

1. over-bureaucratization leads to a state of immobilization.
2. under the disguise of "stabilization" or "consolidation", in reality a standstill takes place which leads to a permanent roll-back process.
3. over-bureaucratization creates an atmosphere of frustration and indifference in the staff towards the cause.
4. bureaucratization hinders future-orientation and makes the institution incapable of competing successfully.

VIII. *Networking*

In the era of globalization, networking is the demand of the hour! In the past, most of the NGOs successfully joined hands with and supported each other, thus creating a functioning networking system without previously naming it so. In the meantime, networking has become a very one-sided affair, as the heavily reduced governmental and international financial support has led to many hardships. In order to exclusively gain from the distributors of grants and subsidies, the NGOs anxiously isolate themselves from each other and try to keep hold onto their benefactors as single darlings.

The following shows our main findings:

1. A certain detachment from previously good relations between different NGOs has taken place, albeit the institutions themselves do not admit it.
2. There are hardly any fresh initiatives of networking within likeminded organisations which might lead to a further weakening of the voluntary sector.
3. The international networking activities have been widely reduced to recruiting new donors and funding organisations instead of exchanging experiences and sharing views, or developing international activities. Thus, the international peace movement with all its implications, among other activities, will have to suffer a further setback.

IX. *Self-sustainability*

We were astonished to notice that very few serious activities had been taken up in the direction of self-sustainability. In view of the fact that since nearly twenty decades, it has been very obvious that Western countries like Germany, France, etc., are cutting down their governmental international economic support budgets as they all were facing economic constraints. The same happened to all half-governmental or private agencies involved in international aid and support work. This process is still continuing and will do so in the foreseeable future. All this has been known very early to all beneficiaries. They seemingly closed eyes and ears and resorted to frantically find new supporters, instead of developing viable strategies of sustainable self-reliance. The writings on the wall have been widely ignored against many warning voices.

The following shows the main findings:

1. No discernible practical steps for self-reliance have been taken, no strategy for developing sustainable, marketable income-generating activities has been developed (nor is it in the pipeline).
2. The fact that governmental and international funding is drastically reduced and also, will continue to do so, is not really recognized.
3. Astonishingly, the practical impacts of globalization have not yet been realized in the planning processes of most of the institutions. We observed evasiveness and a lack of consciousness that funding becomes an issue which can endanger the whole set up.

X. *Marketing*

No proper concept in view of marketing the products is noticeable. In fact, in a few cases where marketing concepts combined with quality-improving measures had been developed and submitted to the decision-making bodies, no steps were taken for practise-transfer.

The following shows the main findings :

1. either there is no (systematic and feasible) marketing concept at all or else, existing ones are not put into practise.
2. marketing is uderstood as merely "selling" products, leading to haphazardly, accidental selling or just relying on age-old relations with some customers which may or may not be stable in the future.
3. no customer-orientation in the sense of reliable servicing or reliability in delivering (time-wise, quality-wise).
4. no innovations are taking place (lack of driving forces for innovation and creativity).

XI. *Summary*

We are of the opinion the mindset and attitudes are determining the performance of individuals and also, of the institutions they work for. Thus, from all the above mentioned findings, we stress upon the attitudinal aspect as all the other findings can be easily improved by reorganising, training, identifying and developing hidden potentials, etc. But, positive, action-oriented mindset and attitude to work and mission are the basic requirements for success.

In the case evaluated by us, it is fact that consciously or unconsciously, people are employed who are deliberately exploiting and harming the NGO; logically, it means that the people responsible for the institutions are supporting this. How is that possible?

There are many factors leading to such a state, among them is an attitude of leniency towards people's behaviour and also, no effecient decision-making takes place which would put the foot down on unwanted activities. There is no practical work evaluation to speak of and, worst of all, if there is the proof that there are non-performance (or bad performance) or harmful activities, no consequences are taken up whatsoever.

The real harm lies in the message which is given to the people, worst of all the young employees, namely, that you can do whatever you want to, even exploiting and harming the institution, and you not only get away with it but also, you will be awarded by your salary. This again, leads to a change in behaviour in those who are trying their best to do their work properly; they start to contemplate about why should they put so much effort in their work if others who do not are not only not taken to task but also rewarded and treated the same? A massive de-motivation process takes place exposing at the same time, poor leadership. Under the excuse or disguise of **consolidation,** the whole infrastructure can come to a stand-still which means that it is not a consolidating process but a continous roll-back, thus extermely harmful to a institution.

Irmel Marla

Internationales Institut für holistische Forschung und Aktion (Germany) (IIHFA)
(International Institute for holistic Research and Voluntary Action) (IIHRVA)

I. ***Aims and Objectives***

Propagating and practising international co-operation with holistic outlook and approach on all issues related to rural development through workshops, seminars, research, and turnkey consultancy. The institute is actively promoting international networking, supporting all efforts for global peace and understanding.

HQ is in Germany; its Indian branch is working simultaneously.

II. ***Main activities/priorities***

1. Establishing close international co-operation with companies, NGOs, Panchyats, academic institutions and persons working on the same lines.
2. Exchanging findings of respective research activities and also, evaluate them (s."aims & objectives": workshops and seminars), exchanging practical experiences with all co-operating partners and others interested.
3. Propagating holistic approach to research and action and all other activities; offering trainings on methods of holistic approach.
4. Conducting international seminars in Germany and India, inviting grassroot experts to share experiences and to learn from each other.
5. Conducting research on holistic rural development in India, also: developing holistic methodology, and synergize activities.

6. Develop "grant-less" concepts for self-employment, enhancing productivity by applying eco-friendly ways and means and/or producing eco-friendly goods, efficient marketing strategies, environment protection.
7. Offering professional turnkey consultancy (for **holistic**: self-employment, enhancing productivity, environment protection, educational and vocational training systems, identifying hidden, unused, unmarketed etc.) potential.

IIHFA Germany	**IIHRVA** India
Irmel Marla, Vorsitzende	**Irmel Marla, Chairperson**
Westenstrasse 2, 76297	Sigmund-Lehmann-Nivas, Mitraniketan
Stutensee, Germany	Vellanad – 695 543, Kerala, India
.Tel. 0049 (0)7244 92379	Phone 0091 (0)472 2883605,
Handy 0049 (0)1749770542	Mob. 9847639624

Indo-German Consultancy

on Gandhian lines

with emphasis on action-oriented Rural Development and Environment Protection

for

- NGOs & Small enterprises
- Govt. institutions/organisations

International Institute for Holistic Research and Voluntary Action, India,

&

Internationales Institut für Holistische Forschung und Aktion, Germany

> "What is productivity but making the most of one's time and talent, and energising the whole surrounding environment so that men and women are inspired and motivated: that is make the most themselves, both as individuals and as members of society on all planes of living, thinking and acting: whether it is politics or economics or home, village or factory, life at the ground level or life of the spirit."
>
> *(Mahatma Gandhi)*

International Standing

INDIA

GERMANY

In view of the overall impact of globalisation on world economies, we offer holistic consultancy for sustainable development by taking into consideration the necessities of :

- opening up to world markets,
- evoking awareness about good leadership,
- marketing the unmarketed,
- identifying and developing hidden potentials,
- international cooperation,
- working for international peace and understanding.

Seminar and Workshop groups .

The **Twin-Institutes** in India and Germany provide the unique features of closely connecting different markets and cultures in an efficient way, thus bringing about better understanding, good co-operation and sustainable growth to the advantage of both the sides.

Aims and Objectives

Propagating and practising international co-operation with holistic outlook and approach on all issues related to rural development through workshops, seminars, research, and turnkey consultancy. The institute is actively promoting international networking, supporting all efforts for global peace and understanding.

HQ is in Germany; its Indian branch is working simultaneously.

Main activities/priorities

1. Establishing close international co-operation with companies, NGOs, Panchyats, academic institutions and persons working on the same lines.
2. Exchanging findings of respective research activities and also, evaluate them ("aims and objectives": workshops and seminars), exchanging practical experiences with all cooperating partners and others interested.

3. Propagating holistic approach to research and action and all other activities; offering trainings on methods of holistic approach.
4. Conducting international seminars in Germany and India, inviting grass root experts to share experiences and to learn from each other.
5. Conducting research on holistic rural development in India, also: developing holistic methodology, and synergize activities.
6. Develop "grant-less" concepts for self-employment, enhancing productivity by applying eco-friendly ways and means and/or producing eco-friendly goods, efficient marketing strategies, environment protection.
7. Offering professional turnkey consultancy (for holistic: self-employment, enhancing productivity, environment protection, educational and vocational training systems, identifying hidden, unused, unmarketed potential, institution building.

The Consultants at work

The Institutes will provide services and conduct Seminars and workshops both, in India and Germany, on

- ***Cross culture issues*** (for managers and officials dealing with European counterparts)
- ***Turnkey consultancy*** (for NGOs, small enterprises, entrepreneurs about to set up an enterprise, and Government administrators)
- ***Monitoring and evaluation services to enhance efficiency*** (for all types of institutions/organisations)
- ***Organisation Development***

- ***Marketing strategies*** (marketing the unmarketed, identifying hidden potentials in personnel and products)
- ***Identifying and connecting business partners internationally***
- ***All fields of human resource development*** (like Leadership training, Work Evaluation methods, personality building, etc.)
- ***Bridging gaps*** between countries, based on Gandhian philosophy
- Disseminating world-wide the ***message of peace and worldwide understanding.***

All activities are designed from a holistic point of view, taking into consideration both, material and immaterial impacts in all the social and business spheres.

Scientists and experienced trainers, consultants and fieldworkers from **East** and **West**, affiliated with the Institutes will share their knowledge and experiences with the participants.

Example for Target Groups:

Women's Self-Help Group

Local Seminars/Workshops in rural surroundings

Commitment to Nature: Imli-Flower

Programmes (selected)

- Seminar on cross-cultural issues for Indian Managers

  * Dealing with German Partners
  * (Do's + Dont's + Exercises)
  * General introduction in German culture and traditions

- Turnkey Consultancy for self-employment and small enterprises, NGOs, public-private enterprises
- Monitoring, Evaluating
- Complete spectre of HRD Tools
- Work Evaluation (tools)
- Marketing the Unmarketed
- Institution Building, Organisation Development
- International Connections
- Gandhian Philosophy in Modern Times

Appendix-II

Holistic Module System for Leadership Training

The **Holistic Module System** is proved to be of great value for practice-oriented and target-oriented trainings; its greatest advantages are :

- High flexibility
- Adjustable to all levels of leadership training (like: beginners middle and top level managers already experienced in leadership tasks)
- Time-saving through tailor-made modules (all modules can be compatibly combined)
- Time-saving through possibility of attending single modules (time-wise intervals) or attending different modules at one stretch
- Highly practice-oriented through workshop-like character of training methods, thus easily transferable into the respective fields of work.

The **12-Modules Training System** can be extended any time according to the needs of the respective organisation.

Training modules

1. **Holistic Mindset and attitudes** towards leadership (making acquainted with holistic approach and issues, assessing abilities in individual personality structures, like empathy, communication, self-initiative, self-discipline, creativity power, etc.).
2. **Work efficiency:** time-economy, decision-making, systematizing work processes, work discipline, systematized planning and performance (responsibilities, milestone method, etc.).

3. **Self-evaluation and self-grading** (incl. assessment of actual knowledge, skills and performance, tools for self-assessment, bench-marking, etc.).
4. **Basic Assessment of key-potential for leadership** in participants (beginners).
5. **Overall assessment of key-potential for leadership** potential in participants already having experience in leadership tasks (incl. assessment for potential of higher (top) leadership positions).
6. **Motivation** (incl. self-motivation, dealing with under-performers, "trouble-makers", etc.).
7. **Negotiating, discussing and debating** (incl. time-saving methods of systematizing, structurizing aim-oriented meetings, convincing skills, evolving creativity and innovative ideas, raising level of debates, etc., this module can be extended to "cross-culture training, i.e. intended to train for dealing with international customers or contacts/agencies).
8. **Quality management as a mindset** (incl. "striving for excellence", "continuous improvement processes" (CIP), reliability in production, customer-oriented production, bench-marking, etc.).
9. **Personnel development** (incl. issues of self-empowerment, self-reliance, leader as change agent, etc.).
10. **Work evaluation** (time-saving tools, qualitative methods leading to practical results and solutions).
11. **Personnel recruitment** (incl. possibilities of approaching prospective candidates, time-saving tools for assessing suitability of candidates, easy decision-making, etc.).
12. **Work efficiency:** time-economy, decision-making, systematizing work processes, work discipline, systematized planning and performance (responsibilities, milestone method, etc.).

Leadership training for leaders in the fields of rural development require mainly the modules dealing with self-assessment, motivation issues, quality awareness, and the practical tools concerning assessments and solutions.

The 12-Modules-System for Leadership Training
- shown with timings -

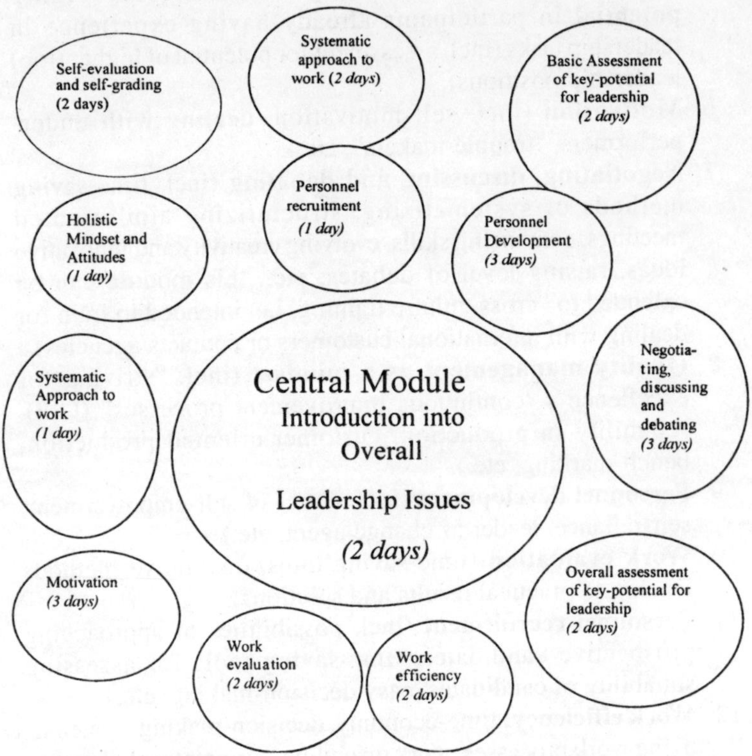

GLOSSARY

CtoCCCB	Charity to Creativity, Capacity and Confidence Building
ICT	Information Communication Technology

Model of analysis for Employment, Investment, Warning and Policy (EIWP):

HIPPOO	Hidden Investible Potential Power of Organisation
KIPPOO	Known Investible Potential Power of Organisation
PIPPOO	Practised Investible Potential Power of Organisation
TIPPOO	Threatening Investible Potential Power of Organisation
FIPPOO	Frightening Investible Potential Power of Organisation
GIPPOO	Globalizationally Investible Power of Organisation
DIPPOO	Disastrously Investible Potential Power of Organisation
$P^4OM^2T^2EC^2$	Philosophy, Planning, Production, Processes, Organizership, Marketing, Management, Training, Technology, Extension, Consultancy, Coordination
RIIGS	Rural Infrastructure and Investment Galvanizing Services
ROI	Return On Investment
SBDC	Small Business Development Centre
SECA	Self Employed Change Agent
SEOE	Self Employed Organizing Entrepreneur
SOPPP	Series of Productive Performer's Presentation
TKC	TurnKey Consultancy
VEC	Village Energy Consultant
VOFC	Village Organic Farming Consultant

Bibliography

Sources of knowledge and enlightenment for the authors

Abraham, J. H.: *Origins and Growth of Sociology*. Penguin, UK, 1977

Aiyappan, Ayinpalli: *Social Revolution in a Kerala Village* (1905). Asia Publishing House, London, 1965

Ali Baig, Tara: *Women of India* (Editor). The Publications Division Govt. of India, 1958

Allison, W. L.: *The Sadhs*. The Religious Life of India Series. Y.M.C.A. Publishing House, Calcutta, 1935

Amnesty International Report, 1981

Andrews, Robert Hardy: *A Lamp for India. The Story of Madame Pandit*. Arthur Barker Ltd., London, 1967

Atkinson, John, W.; *Motives in Fansy, Action and Society*, D. Van Nostrand Company, Inc., New Jersly (New Delhi), 1966

Baden-Powell, B. H.: *The Origin and Growth of Village Communities in India*. Swan Sonnenschein & Co., (1899), reprint 1970

Balaram, N. E.: *A Short History of the Communist Party of India*. Prabhath Book House, Trivandrum, 1967

Barghava, G. S.: *Indira's India Gate*. Arnold-Heinemann Publishers India, New Delhi, 1977

Basham, A. L.: *The Wonder that was India*. Fontana Books in Ass. With Rupa & Co., Calcutta, 1967

Basu, Priya: *Improving Access to Finance for India's Rural Poor*. The World Bank Publications, Washington, 2006

Baviskar B. S.: *The Politics of Development*, Oxford University Press, Bombay, 1980

Becsi, Kurt: *Das Indische Zeitalter. Perspektiven und Profile*. Europaverlag, 1973

Beteille, Andre & Madan, T. N. (Editors): *Encounter and Experience. Personal Accounts of Fieldwork*. Vikas Publishing House Pvt. Ltd., 1975

Bhave, Vinoba:

- *Bhoodan Yojna.* Navajivan Publishing House, Ahmedabad, 1957
- *Swaraj Sastra.* Sarva Seva Sangh Prakashan, Varanasi, 1963

Bhyrappa, S.L.: *Vamshavriksha.* Sri Venkatesa Printing House, Madras, 1995D.

Paul Chowdhry: *Profile of Voluntary Action in Social Welfare and Development.* Siddartha Publishers, New Delhi, ISBN-81-85464-01-4

Bipan Chandra: *Communalism in Modern India.* Vikas Publishing House, 1984, reprint 1992

Bose, Nirmal Kumar: *Gandhiji. The Man and his Mission.* Bharatiya Vidya Bhavan. Bombay, 1966

Brox, Ottar: *The Political Economy of Rural Development. Modernisation without Centralisation*? Eburon Academic Publishers, Delft, Netherlands, 2006

Buehler, Georg (Translator into English): *The Laws of Manu*, Best Books, 1986

Chaliand, Gerard: *The Peasants of Vietnam.* Penguin UK, 1969

Carrington, Richard: *A Million Years of Man.* Weidenfeld & Nicolson, London, 1963

Challenge of Poverty and the Gandhian Answer (Reader). Sarva Seva Sangh Prakashan, Varanasi, 1973

Dagli, Vadilal (Editor): *India and Germany. A Survey of Economic Relations.* Vora & Co. Publishers Pvt. Ltd., Bombay, 1970

Dayal, John and Bose, Ajoy: *For Reasons of State. Delhi under Emergency.* Ess Ess Publications, New Delhi, 1977

Dennett, Daniel C.: *Darwin's Dangerous Idea. Evolution and the Meanings of Life.* Simon & Schuster, New York, 1995

Dharampal: *Civil Disobedience and Indian Tradition.* Sarva Seva Sangh Prakashan, Varanasi, 1971

Dilenschneider, Robert L.: *A Briefing for Leaders. Communication as the Ultimate Exercise of Power.* Harper Business, HarperCollins Publications, 1992

Diwarkar, R. R.: *Saga of Satyagraha.* Gandhi Peace Foundation, New Delhi, 1969

Durga Das: *India from Curzon to Nehru & after.* Rupa & Co. Collins, 1974

Dutt, Romesh: *The Economic History of India*, Vol. I and II, Publications Division, New Delhi, 1989

Duus, Peter : *Fedralism in Japan.* Studies in World Civilization. Alfred A. Knopf, New York, 2nd ed., 1976

Empowerment through Enterprise. A training manual for NGOs, Malcolm Harper, Oxford & IBH Co.Pvt. Ltd., New Delhi, 1995

Fanon, Frantz: *Toward the African Revolution*. Penguin Books, London, 1970

Firth, Raymond: *Elements of Social Organization*. Josiah Maon Lectures delivered at the University of Birmingham. Beacon Press, Boston, 3rd ed., 1966

Fraser, Thomas M. Jr.: *Culture and Change in India. The Barpali Experiment*. University of Massachusetts Press, 1968

Gandhi, M. K.:

- *From Yeravda Mandir*. Navajivan Publishing House, Ahmedabad, 1957
- *Hind Swaraj or Indian Home Rule*, Navajivan Publishing House, Ahmedabad, 2005
- *India of my Dreams*. (Compiled by R.K. Prabhu). Navajivan Publishing House, Ahmedabad, 1970
- *Non-Violence in Peace & War*. Vol. I, Navajivan Publishing House, Ahmedabad, 1962
- *Rebuilding our Villages*. Navajivan Publishing House, Ahmedabad, 2nd reprint, 1969
- *Sarvodaya*. (Wohlfahrt für alle). Edit. Bharatan Kumarappan, translated into German by Karl Mueller. Hinder + Deelmann, Gladenbach, 2nd ed., 1975
- *Self-Restraint v. Self-Indulgence*. Navajivan Publishing House, Ahmedabad, (1928), 1969
- *Strikes* (compiled by Ravindra Kelekar), Navajivan Publishing Hourse, Ahmedabad, 1961
- *The Supreme Power*, (edit. and published by Anand T. Hingorani) Pearl Publications Pvt. Ltd., Bombay, 1963

Hardgrave, Robert L., Jr.: *The Dravidian Movement*. Popular Prakashan, Bombay, 1986

Hirway, Indira, Cottin, Jacqui, Pushkar Pandya: *Towards Eradication of Child Labour*. Gandhi Labour Institute, Ahmedabad, 1991

Holland, John H.: *Hidden Order: How Adaptation Builds Complexity*. Perseus Books, 1995

Indian Society: *Historical Probings*. In Memory of D. D. Kosambi. Edited by R. S. Sharma. People's Publishing House, New Delhi, 1977

India's Environment. Crises and Responses. Edited by: J. Banyopadhyay, N. D. Jayal, U. Schoettli, Chhatrapati Singh. Natraj Publishers, Dehra Dun, 1985

India's Foreign Policy and the Unipolar World. In: *Social Action.* A Quarterly Review of Social Trends, Vol. 42, No. 3, 1992, published by Indian Social Institute, New Delhi

Jain, Devaki (Editor): *Indian Women.* Publications Division, Ministry of Information and Broadcasting, Govt. of India, 1975

Jha, M. L.: *Untouchability and Education.* Namita Publications, Meerut, 1973

Jain, R. B. and Chaudhuri, P. N.: *Bureaucratic Values in Development.* Uppal Publishing House, New Delhi, 1982

Jalan, Bimal (Editor): *The Indian Economy. Problems and Prospects.* Viking Penguin India, New Delhi, 1992

Johnson, Phyllis and Martin, David (editors) : *Destructive Engagement Southern Africa at War*, Zimbabwe Publishing House, Harare, 1986

Jones, Morgan D.: *The Thinker's Toolkit: 14 Powerful Techniques for Problem Solving.* Random House, 1998

Kellenbenz, Hermann: *Deutsche Wirtschaftsgeschichte*, Band I. Von den Anfaengen bis zum Ende des 18. Jahrhunderts. C. H. Beck, Muenchen, 1977

Khalatbari, Parviz: *Oekonomische Unterentwicklung. Mechanismus—Problem - Ausweg.* Verlag Marxistische Blätter, Frankfurt/Main, 1972

Kim, S. K.: *The Philosophical Thoughts of Mahatma Gandhi.* Vikas Publishing House Pvt. Ltd., 1996

Kohli, Atul: *Democracy and Discontent. India's Growing Crisis of Governability.* Cambridge University Press, 1991

Kray, John: *History of India*, Hyper Collins, London/India, 2000

Kripalani, Krishna (compiled and edited): *All Men are Brothers.* Life and Thoughts of Mahatma Gandhi as told in his own words. Navajivan Publishing House, Ahmedabad, 1971

Krishna, Nandita: *The Book of Vishnu.* Viking Penguin Books, India, New Delhi, 2001

Krishna Rao, Y. V.: *Growth of Capitalism in Agriculture. A Case Study of Andhra Pradesh.* Visalaandhra Publishing House, 1984

Krueger, Horst; Heidrich, Joachim; Weidemann, Diethelm, Carpin, Jochen: *Indien in der Welt von heute.* Staatsverlag der DDR, Berlin, 1972

Kumar, Kapil: *Peasants in Revolt. Tenants, Landlords, Congress and the Raj in Oudh.* Manohar Publications, New Delhi, 1984

Kumarappa, J. C.: *Swaraj for the Masses.* Srava Seva Sangh Prakashan, Kashi, 1958

Kureishi, Hanif: *The Buddha of Suburbia.* Faber & Faber, London, 1990

Land to the Tiller. A Publication by the Department of Public Relations of Govt. of Kerala, 1971

Leela, S.: *Fables from the Panchatantra.* India Book House Education Trust Bombay, 4th ed., 1973

Leifer, Walter: *India and the Germans. 500 years of Indo-German Contacts.* Shakuntala Publishing House, 1971

Leipold, Helmut: *Alternative Gesellschafts- and Wirtschaftssysteme.* Grundzuege einer Theorie des Systemvergleichs. Hrsg.: Niedersaechsische Landeszentrale fuer Politische Bildung, 1974

Lewis, Norman: *A Goddess in the Stones.* Jonathan Cape, London, 1991

Marla, V. Sarma: *Bonded Labour in India.* Biblia Impex Pvt. Ltd., New Delhi, 1981

Mehta, Ramanlal V.: *A Thesis on The Legal Rights of Women under Different Communal Laws in Vogue in India.* The Advocate of India Press, Bombay, 1933

Marx, Karl/Engels, Friedrich: *On Colonialism.* Progress Publishers, Moscow, 1968

Menon, V. P.: *The Transfer of Power in India.* Orient Longmans, New Delhi, 1968

Meredith, Martin: *The First Dance of Freedom. Black Africa in the Post-war Era.* Abacus Sphere Books, London, 1985

Millonig, Harald; Olsson, Elisabeth; Pflug, Bernd; Scheel, Bernd: *Indien. Argumente und Thesen in der Erwachsenenbildung.* In: Materialien 5, VHS und der Themenbereich Afrika-Asien-Lateinamerika, Deutscher Volkshochschul-Verband e.V., 1978

Mitra, Pratap and Sen, Mohit : *Communist Party and Naxalites,* Communist Party Publication, New Delhi, 1971

M. L. Dantwala: *Poverty in India—then and now 1870-1970.* Macmillan India, Madras, 1973

Moddie, A. D: *The Brahmanical Culture and Modernity.* Asia Publishing House, 1968

Mohan Ram: *Maoism in India.* Vikas Publications, New Delhi, 1971

Mohanti, Prafulla: *My Village, My Life.* Corgi Books, London, 1975

Moorhouse, Geoffrey: *India Britannica*, Paladin Books, Granada Publ. Ltd., London, 1984

Mueller, Max: *Introduction to the Science of Religion*. Four Lectures. Bharata Manisha, 1st Indian Reprint 1972

Mukherjee, Prabhati: *Hindu Women. Normative Models*. Orient Longman Ltd., New Delhi, 1978

Mukherjee, Ramkrishna: *The Dynamics of a Rural Society*. Akademie-Verlag Berlin, 1957

Mukherjee, Sadhan: *Who Really Aids India—USA or USSR*? A Communist Party Publication, New Delhi, 1972

Naipaul, V. S.: *India. A Million Mutinies Now*. Minerva, London, 1990

Nair, P. T.: *Marriage and Dowry in India*. Minerva Associates Publ. Pvt. Ltd., Calcutta, 1978

Namboodiripad, E. M. S.: *Conflicts and Crisis*. Political India: 1974. Sangam Books, Pune, 1974

Narasimham, C. : *Me and My Times*, Radna Corporation, Hyderabad, 1986

Narayan, Jayaprakash: *Total Revolution*. Sarva Seva Sangh Prakashan, 1975

Narayan, R. K.:

- *Grandmother's Tale*. Indian Thought Publications, Madras, 1992
- *Mr. Sampath*. Hind Pocket Books, New Delhi, 1979
- *My Days. A Memoir*. Indian Thought Publications, Mysore, 1975

Natwar-Singh, K. (Editor): *Stories from India*. B. I. Publications, New Delhi, 1972

Nayar, Kuldip:

- *Between the Lines*. Hind Pocket Books Ltd., 6th ed., 1971
- *India. The Critical Years*. Vikas Publications, New Delhi, 1971
- *The Judgement. Inside Story of the Emergency in India*. Vikas Publications, New Delhi, 1977

Nehru, Jawaharlal: *The Discovery of India*. Asia Publishing House, 1960

Palkhivala, N. A.: *Our Constitution. Defaced and Defiled*. Macmillan India, 1974

Paul F. Secord, Carl W. Backman: *Social Psychology.* McGraw-Hill Book Company, New York, 1964

People's Publishing House, New Delhi (Editorial Committee): *Society and Revolution. Essays in Honour of Engels.* 1970

Pigott, Stuart: *Some Ancient Cites of India.* Geoffrey Cumberlege Oxford University Press, London, 1945

Prabhu, R. K., and Rao, U. R. (compiled and edited): *The Mind of Mahatma Gandhi*, Navajivan Publishing House, Ahmedabad, 1969

Prasad, Nageshwar : *Decentralisation in Yugoslavia and India,* Navachetna Prakashan, Varanasi, 1972

Prasad, R. C.: *Democracy and Development. The Grass-Roots Experience in India.* Rachna Prakashan, New Delhi, 1971

Pyarelal: *Mahatma Gandhi. The Last Phase.* Vol. I and II, Navajivan Publishing House, Ahmedabad, 1958

Radhakrishnan, Sarvepalli and Moore, Charles A. (Editors): *A Source Book in Indian Philosophy.* Princeton University Press, 1960

Rajagopalachari, C. (transl.): *Mahabharata.* Bharatiya Vidya Bhavan, Bombay, 1973

Ram, Suresh: *Vinoba and His Mission.* Akhil Bharat Sarva Seva Sangh, Kashi, 1958

Roberts, P.E.: *History of British India*, Surjeet Publications, First Indian Reprint, 2004

Rodney, Walter : *How Europe underdeveloped Africa Zimbabwe.* Publishing House, Harare, 1981

Russell, Bertrand: *A History of Western Philosophy.* Simon & Schuster, New York, 1964

Sardesai, S. G. (Editor):

- *India and the Russian Revolution.* Communist Party Publication, New Delhi, 1967
- *Problems of Peace and Socialism*, Vol. I, Sept. 1973

Sartre, Jean-Paul: *Being and Nothingness.* Washington Square Press, New York, 2nd ed., 1970

Sastri, Chatterjee Heramba: *The Social Background of the Forms of Marriage in Ancient India*, Vol. II. Sanskrit Pustak Bhandar, Calcutta, 1974

Sawyer, Roger : *Slaveryin the Turntieth Century.* Routledge and Kegan Paul, 1986

Segal, Ronald: *The Crisis of India.* Jaico Publishing House, Bombay, 1968

Selbourne, David: *An Eye to India. The Unmasking of a Tyranny.* Penguin, UK, 1977

Sen, Sunil: *Agrarian Relations in India 1793—1947.* People's Publishing House, New Delhi, 1979

Shah, K. T. (Editor): *Women's Role in Planned Economy.* Report of the Sub-Committee, National Planning Committee Series, Vora & Co., Publishers Ltd., 1947

Shah, S. A. (Editor): *India : Degradation & Development.* Parts I and II. M. Venkatarangaiya Foundation, 1982

Sharma, Pratap: *Days of the Turban.* India Book Distributors, Bombay, 1996

Shirer, William L.: *Gandhi. A Memoir.* Washington Square Press, New York, 1982

Shourie, Arun: *Worshipping False Gods.* Ambedkar, and the facts which have been erased. Harper Collins Publishers India, 1999

Singh, Kushwant: *Train to Pakistan.* Pearl Book, 3rd ed., 1970

Singh, Randir: *Reason, Revolution and Political Theory.* People's Publishing House, New Delhi, 1967

Singham, A. W. & Hune, Shirley: *Non-Alignment in an Age of Alignments.* The College Press, London, 1986

Sinha, B. M.: *Operation Emergency.* Hind Pocket Books, New Delhi, 1977

Sinha, Sachhidanand: *The Internal Colony. A Study in Regional Exploitation.* Sindhu Publications, New Delhi, 1973

Social Scientist, Monthly Journal of the Indian School of Social Sciences, Vol. 8, No. 12, July, 1980

Srinivas, M. N., Seshaiah, S., Parthasarathy, V. S.: *Dimensions of Social Change in India.* Allied Publishers Pvt. Ltd., 1978

Subrahmanyam, Subhashini Y.: *Social Change in Village India. An Andhra Case Study.* Prithvi Raj Publishers, New Delhi, 1975

Swift, Jonathan: *Gulliver's Travels.* Victor Pettersons Borkindustriakt Ebolag, Stockholm, 1947

Tagore, Rabindranath: *A Vision of India's History.* Published for Visva-Bharati by Prabhatchandra Ray, Calcutta, 1951

Tajfel, Henri and Fraser, Collin: *Introducing Social Psychology,* Penguin Books, England, 1978

Taori, Kamal (Vidyarthi):

- *Disaster Management Through Panchayati Raj*. Concept Publishing Company, New Delhi, 2005
- *Marketing North East*. Compiled and collated together with Siddharth Sharma. National Productivity Council, New Delhi, 2006-12-08
- *Marketing the Unorganised Sector. Issues, Perspectives and Strategies*. Concept Publishing Company, New Delhi, 2003
- *People's Participation in Sustainable Human Development* (A Unified Search). Concept Publishing Company, New Delhi, 1998
- *Sustainable Human Development. Issues and Challenges*. Concept Publishing Company, New Delhi, 2000
- & Surendra Singh: *Rural Industrialisation. A Plan for the Future*. Vikas Publishing House Pvt. Ltd., 2nd ed., 1995

Tendulkar, D. G.: *Mahatma. Life of Mohandas Karamchand Gandhi*. Vol. 8, 1947-1948. The Publications Division, Ministry of Information and Broadcasting, Govt. of India, 1963

Thackersey, Premilla: *Education of Women. A Key to Progress*. Publication of Ministry of Education & Youth Services Govt. of India, 1970

Thapar, Romila: History and Beyond. Oxford University Press, New Delhi, 2002

Third World Chronicle. An International Quaterly for Developing Countries, Politica Verlag, Munich, No. 2, 1976.

Thottam, P. J.: *Modernising Ayurveda*. Sura Books Pvt. Ltd., Chennai, 2005

Trivedi, Harshad R.: *Scheduled Caste Women Studies in Exploitation. With Reference to Superstition, Ignorance and Poverty*. Concept Publishing Company, New Delhi, 1977

Ulyanovsky, R., Pavlov, V.: *Asian Dilemma. A Soviet View and Myrdal's Concept*. Progress Publishers, Moscow, 1973

Varma, Pavan K.: *The Book of Krishna*, Viking Penguin India, New Delhi, 2001

Venkatacharya, Prativadi Bhayankara: *Craik's Paradise. Life in the Andamans*. 1938

Verma, Mukut Behari (compiled in Hindi): *History of the Harijan Sevak Sangh 1932-1968*, published by Harijan Sevak Sangh, New Delhi, 1971

Vidyarthi, L. P. (Editor): *Applied Anthropology in India*. Kitab Mahal, Allahabad

Vidyarthi, L. P., Sahay, B. N., Srivastava, B. R. (Editors): *Gandhi and Social Sciences*. Bookhive Publishers & Booksellers, New Delhi, 1970

Vikram Seth: *A Suitable Boy*. Viking Penguin Books India, 1993

Weidenreich, Franz: *Apes, Giants and Man*, University of Chicago Press, Chicago, 1946

Whitehead, Henry: *The Village Gods of South India*. Association Press, Calcutta, 1921

Woodruff, Philip: *The Men Who Ruled India*. Vol. II, The Guardians. Jonathan Cape, London, 1971

World Commission on Environment and Development (Editors): *Our Common Future* (Reader), Oxford University Press, New Delhi, 2nd ed., 1987

INDEX